SECRET MEMPHIS

A GUIDE TO THE WEIRD,

WONDERFUL, AND OBSCURE

Holly R. Whitfield

Library of Congress Control Number: 2019936722

ISBN: 9781681062327

Design by Jill Halpin

Printed in the United States of America
20 21 22 23 24   5 4 3 2

DEDICATION

For my family and my friends, with love.
For Memphis, a city full of secrets worth sharing.

CONTENTS

ACKNOWLEDGMENTS

I want to thank my parents, Bonnie and George, who have encouraged my many "projects" since I was a small child, and my brother Christopher, who is supportive when I need it most and who is the first person to read this, my first book. To my chosen family: Abby, Ace, Allie, Katie, Matthew, Meghan, Melissa, Samantha, and Sarah. Thank you for encouraging me and celebrating with me throughout the *Secret Memphis* process.

To all of my work family at Memphis Tourism: Thank you for supporting me professionally and personally, thank you for enabling my love for Memphis, and for being excited about this book. To Jan Coleman: Thank you for telling me I could do this so many years ago.

To my extended family, my friends, and my fellow Memphis lovers: Thank you for all your encouraging messages, enthusiasm, ideas, and reassurance. To the Wiffle Ballers and to Tyler and Scott: I appreciate you. To I Love Memphis Blog readers: Y'all are the best. Thank you for sharing your passion for Memphis with me.

Throughout my research, many people kindly shared their stories, their time, and their knowledge. I'd like to thank Savannah Shelton from the Green Beetle family, John Curran and Meghan Stuthard from St. Jude, Michael Detroit and Marcus Cox from Playhouse on the Square, Jeff Hulett, Rocky Kasaftes from Alex's, Kristin Bennett from the Orpheum Theatre, Marvin Stockwell and the Coliseum Coalition, the Wolf River Conservancy, Mary Helen Butler from the Memphis Botanic Garden, Angie Whitfield and Rebecca Dailey from

Shelby Farms Park, Carolyn Michael-Banks and A Tour of Possibilities, Kristen Rambo from the Dixon Gallery & Garden, J. Dylan Sandifer from Rhodes College, John Younger and the crew at Altown DIY Skatepark, artist Michael Roy, John Miller from Shangri-La Records, Patrick Glass and the team at Memphis Record Pressing, Joseph Miner, Jayne Ellen White, Sam Shansky and the team at DittyTV, Lindsey Jenkins, Vance Lauderdale, Rebecca Phillips and Caitlin Horton of Memphis Type History.

INTRODUCTION

Memphis is a city that changes the world, and Memphians from every generation have impacted culture through music, history, science, art, cuisine, and more. Its stories and secrets are endless and would take a lifetime to discover and unravel. I knew from the beginning this book couldn't cover every Memphis secret, but that it could be the perfect start to a Memphis exploration.

Secret Memphis is a book for lifelong Memphians, for recent transplants to the city, for people planning a visit, and for folks who don't know a thing about Memphis besides the fact that Graceland is here. With this in mind, I took a few approaches in choosing which Memphis secrets to feature. In some cases, we'll uncover surprising tidbits and hidden sites full of shocking history. Other times, this book reveals the anecdotes and drama behind Memphis's most prominent landmarks, famous places, and oddities. For example, you may be aware that there's a giant glass pyramid downtown, but *Secret Memphis* gives you a behind-the-scenes look into the who, what, when, and why. After all, in Memphis there are as many skeletons in the closet as there are delightful gems to discover.

This book is a different kind of travel guide, full of exciting twists and unexpected turns. It's a look at the city's sometimes difficult past, while appreciating the soul that makes the city unique. Above all, it's a love letter to Memphis. I hope you fall for Memphis as much as I have.

HIDDEN CEMETERY IN MIDTOWN

Why is there a graveyard next to a grocery store?

In 1818 Tillman and Sally Bettis settled on sprawling farmland in what is now Midtown, just one year before the city's official charter. They were the second family of white settlers to call Memphis home, and Tillman served as the first school commissioner in the territory. Several generations of the Bettis family enjoyed birth, life, and burial on the farm, but all that's left now is the Bettis Family Cemetery, a Memphis mystery hidden in plain sight. Locals pass by constantly, but most of us have forgotten about it, if we ever knew of it at all.

Even if you expect it, the sight of a quiet little graveyard between a Cash Saver grocery and a Home Depot can surprise you. The eroding earth has cracked several of the gravestones and toppled the small obelisk that once stood

BETTIS FAMILY CEMETERY

What: A secret graveyard in the middle of the city

Where: 56 Angelus St.

Cost: Free

Pro tip: The Cash Saver grocery store next to the cemetery has a great selection of local and craft beer.

Stumble upon the oldest-known gravesite in Shelby County; it's next to a big-box store and a grocery in the heart of Midtown.

The historical marker is the only way to see the Bettis plot from the street, as most of the gravestones have tumbled over.

This is what's left of the small tower that marked Tillman Bettis's grave, which says he was born on October 6, 1788, and died on February 9, 1854.

to honor Tillman's final resting place. At least eight Bettis family members are thought to be buried here, including his first wife, Sally Carr Bettis, who died giving birth to their ninth child. Sadly, the spot is not well cared for, and you're likely to encounter tall grass and other debris when you're there. It's a monument to nineteenth-century Memphis that's quietly fading away as the city grows and evolves around it, so see it while you can.

PRINCE MONGO'S CASTLE

Who lives in the castle in Midtown?

Who walks around barefoot, ran for mayor a couple of times, is a self-identified extraterrestrial, and once owned a castle in Memphis? Only one citizen can claim this biography, and that's the infamous Prince Mongo. The affluent gentleman (legal name Robert Hodges) is a Memphis personality and the embodiment of eccentricity, often seen wearing goggles and a long blond wig. From 1990 to 2013, he owned a huge mock castle in the Central Gardens neighborhood of Memphis, which he operated as a nightclub called the Castle.

The structure, officially named Ashlar Hall, was built in 1896 by Memphian Robert Brinkley Snowden as the family home. Today the castle still towers above the busy street, covered in gray ashlar stone, with eye-catching crenellated towers, columns, and porticos. In the 1950s the Snowden family sold the castle to the Grisantis, who ran a restaurant in the space. Prince Mongo, who claims to be a resident of the planet Zambodia, took over in 1990 and for several years proceeded to host crazy parties that Memphians still gossip about. In early 2019 a partially renovated Ashlar

---

ASHLAR HALL

What: A Gothic Revival house that was once a notorious, inglorious nightclub

Where: 1397 Central Ave.

Cost: Free to see; event fees vary

Pro tip: See how many Mongo For Mayor stickers or campaign signs you can spot around town.

The Gothic Revival home is on the western edge of the Central Gardens historic neighborhood.

Hall temporarily reopened to the public for experiential art performances from local production group Lost In Found. While we wait for the home's next life, you can still stop by and see what locals will forever call "Prince Mongo's Castle" for yourself.

In the nineties, the Castle offered twenty-five-cent beers, wet t-shirt contests, and a chance to win tropical getaways to its patrons.

NO MAN'S LAND AT ELMWOOD

Who is buried in "No Man's Land"?

In the 1870s Memphis was a stop along the superhighway of the day: the Mississippi River. Thousands of riverboats traveled between New Orleans and Chicago, stopping in Memphis along the way. The boats carried supplies, food, whiskey, and people across the country. But the boats also brought disease. During the 1800s Memphis experienced six different yellow fever epidemics. The worst was in 1878, when 90 percent of the population contracted the disease and more than five thousand people died. The demand for burial space and graves strained the resources of the city's cemeteries, including Elmwood Cemetery. Elmwood, which is home to war heroes, mayors, and prominent citizens, also had separate plots for poor and unidentified people. In a rush to lay the yellow fever victims to rest, decorum and

ELMWOOD CEMETERY

What: An anonymous mass grave for yellow fever victims

Where: 824 S. Dudley St.

Cost: Free to visit

Pro tip: The cemetery hosts regular ticketed history tours and fun events to support the upkeep of the grounds.

The simple marker is in stark contrast to the beautiful and elaborate sculptures and memorials that mark the final resting places of the wealthy and powerful buried in other areas of Elmwood.

The No Man's Land marker was erected in 1985. Inset: A wrought iron gate marks the entrance to the historic cemetery.

social order were forgotten. Everyone from the highest society members to anonymous prostitutes were buried together in an anonymous mass grave now called "No Man's Land."

While the majority of the city's residents fled, those who stayed behind had already fallen ill or were among the selfless physicians, nuns, and everyday people who remained to care for the sick. It is believed that many of these people ended up in No Man's Land. Of the twenty-five hundred yellow fever victims buried in Elmwood, about fourteen hundred are buried in the No Man's Land area, which is noted with a marker.

A PINK PALACE

What does Piggly Wiggly have to do with a pink mansion?

In 1916 an eccentric Memphis businessman named Clarence Saunders had a grand idea—what if, instead of people waiting for a shopkeeper to fetch their flour and eggs from behind the counter, they pulled their sundries and supplies from shelves themselves? Thus the modern grocery store was born, and Clarence named it Piggly Wiggly. The origin of the name cannot be definitively traced, but the grocer built the first location on Jefferson Avenue in Memphis, and the concept proved successful.

Using his fortune from these new self-service shops, which he patented and franchised across the country, Clarence set out to build himself a fanciful and spacious mansion built of Georgian pink marble set on a hill in Memphis. In 1923, before he could take up residence in what locals had begun to call "The Pink Palace," he ran into some stock market trouble and suddenly lost his company and his Piggly Wiggly fortune.

The Pink Palace hosts plenty of events in the museum and mansion spaces, from wine education programs to charity parties and holiday celebrations.

The mansion portion of the Pink Palace.

THE PINK PALACE

What: A pink mansion built by the inventor of grocery stores

Where: 3050 Central Ave.

Cost: For museum exhibits, adults, $15; seniors 60+, $14; children 3-12, $10; children 2 and under, free

Pro tip: For a $30 ticket, get access to the museum, the CTI 3D Giant Theater, and the Sharpe Planetarium.

Saunders went on to develop more futuristic grocery concepts and at one point owned a short-lived professional football team in Memphis he named the Clarence Saunders Sole Owner of My Name Tigers. In 1930, the mansion reopened to the public as a museum, which guests can visit today to see artifacts from throughout Memphis history, and other curiosities such as a real shrunken head, an enormous flea circus, and a replica of the original Piggly Wiggly location.

THE GREEN BEETLE

Where is the oldest tavern in Memphis?

If you didn't know any better, you might think that the Green Beetle on South Main was just another neighborhood watering hole. It's an unassuming, welcoming place, with a patio outside and full bar inside. Daily lunch specials, plenty of beer, and a popular Beetle Burger are always on the menu. What you might not know is that the Green Beetle is one of the oldest taverns in Memphis, and it's illegal for any owner, now or in the distant future, to change the bar's name.

In 1939 second-generation Italian-American Frank Liberto opened the Green Beetle just down the street from the Orpheum Theatre and the Chisca Hotel. Let's go back a bit further, though, to an intriguing legend that goes like this: before Frank's Green Beetle, the spot was a speakeasy frequented by Machine Gun Kelly, who is said to have hidden his money somewhere in the building. The tale is that one day, the notorious gangster opened fire, leaving the bar riddled

THE GREEN BEETLE

What: A neighborhood bar with a buggy name

Where: 325 S. Main St.

Cost: Varies

Pro tip: After you've had the burger, try the Green Beetle's weekly plate specials and pick a local brew from its large beer menu.

Hank Williams Sr. was a regular attendee at the Beetle's basement poker games in the forties and fifties.

The Beetle's patio is perfect for a laid-back afternoon meal or an adult beverage.

with bullet holes. Neither money nor bullet holes were ever discovered, but regardless of the legend's merits, the place shaped up into a more legal venture when the Libertos took over. In the 1940s and '50s the Green Beetle was a well-documented popular hangout for celebrities such as Desi Arnaz and Hank Williams Sr.

After Frank passed away in the 1970s, his wife Mary had to sell the buildings, but not before she added a permanent rule to the property's deed: it must always be named the Green Beetle. In 2011 chef Josh Huckaby, grandson of Frank, bought the property back into his family and reopened the bar with plenty of his family's favorite recipes, plus his own modern creations. You can still get a Beetle Burger—and a beer on the cheap too.

THE LABYRINTH BY THE TREE OF LIFE

Where can you walk through a labyrinth in a park?

If you're seeking some solace but don't have time to fully escape the city, make your way through the labyrinth at the Richard and Annette Bloch Cancer Survivors Park in East Memphis, on the east end of Audubon Park. Visitors are encouraged to meander through this two-acre sanctuary, which is home to multiple sculptures and a unique ground labyrinth pathway.

The backdrop for the labyrinth is the colorful *Tree of Life* mosaic, created by local artist Kristi Duckworth. The Cancer Survivors Park includes several other pieces of art. Sculptor Victor Salmones created eight life-size human figures making their way through a maze-like cancer journey, and multiple plaques sharing inspirational quotes are placed throughout the space. The theme of color and peaceful nature continues with wildflower beds and butterfly sculptures from Memphis artist Yvonne Bobo.

This park is part of a series of Cancer Survivors Parks nationwide, all built and maintained by the Richard

CANCER SURVIVORS PARK

What: A peaceful park with a purpose

Where: 701 Perkins Extd.

Cost: Free to visit

Pro tip: Continue your walk through the adjacent Audubon Park, or visit the Memphis Botanic Garden nearby.

The arch mosaic and labyrinth pathway at Cancer Survivors Park.

and Annette Bloch Family Foundation. Each one is specifically designed for its city and location, so the Memphis park is a unique experience.

The artist worked with local cancer survivors and their families to select colorful pieces used in the *Tree of Life* design, which depicts a massive tree surrounded by flora and fauna.

ROBERT CHURCH PARK

Who was the first black millionaire in the United States?

On the east end of Beale Street, in the shadow of the FedExForum arena and surrounded by historic churches, you'll find eight acres of open ground with pavilions and playgrounds designated as Robert R. Church Park.

Robert R. Church was a Memphian of many firsts and singularities. Born in Mississippi, Robert was the son of an enslaved mother and a wealthy white father who never formally recognized or educated his son. Robert worked in his family's steamboat business on the Mississippi River until he was stranded in Memphis during the Civil War after the Union Army captured the boat he was working on.

He never looked back. Robert survived the race riots of 1866, as well as the yellow fever epidemic of 1878, during which Memphis lost most of its population and its city charter. Church was instrumental in reestablishing the city by being the first citizen to purchase a one-thousand-dollar bond

ROBERT R. CHURCH PARK

What: A park commemorating the nation's first black millionaire

Where: Corner of Beale Street and South Fourth Street

Cost: Free

Pro tip: Spend some time in this area—you'll find quite a few of our Memphis secrets nearby.

Robert R. Church Park hosts the Africa in April festival, which honors a different African nation each year through music, food, dancing, and cultural exhibits.

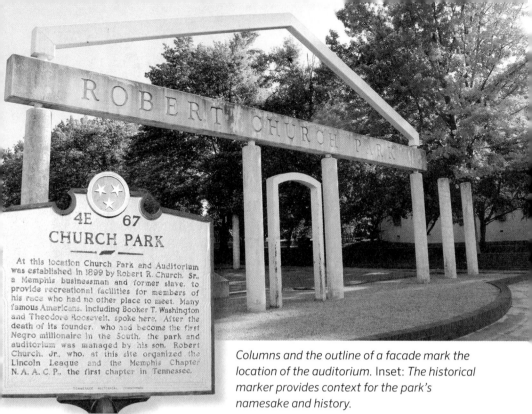

Columns and the outline of a facade mark the location of the auditorium. Inset: The historical marker provides context for the park's namesake and history.

restoring the charter. He bought and developed business property in the struggling city, including hotels, restaurants, saloons, and other establishments on Beale Street, a haven for African Americans.

He became the first black millionaire in the United States, owned the only first-class hotel for African Americans at the time, and founded Solvent Savings Bank and Trust, at one time the largest African American bank in the nation. He built Robert Church Park and Auditorium in 1899, the latter a state-of-the-art venue that boasted blues legend W. C. Handy as its orchestra leader and President Theodore Roosevelt among its guest speakers.

While the auditorium was demolished, you can still walk through this space and recognize Church's dedication to creating safe spaces for black Memphians during a time of segregation, persecution, and violence.

PHILLIPS RECORDING STUDIO

What did Sam Phillips do after Sun Studio?

While millions of visitors flock to Sun Studio to hold the microphone where Elvis crooned his earth-shattering early rock 'n' roll songs, around the corner you'll find the rest of the story. Sam Phillips founded the famous Sun Studio in 1950 (then called Memphis Recording Service) and launched the careers of musicians such as B. B. King, Johnny Cash, Roy Orbison, Carl Perkins, and, of course, Elvis Presley. With his tireless search for fresh sounds and his willingness to record amateur musicians of any race, Phillips kick-started rock 'n' roll as an internationally beloved genre from his home base in Memphis. By 1960 he'd outgrown the space at Sun Studio on Union and opened the state-of-the-art Sam C. Phillips Recording Studio barely a mile away.

The place was fully decked out in sixties mod decor and pastels and featured movable acoustic panels, control rooms, and all the latest technology, plus a snazzy bar and lounge. Even after Phillips sold Sun Records in 1969, he continued to operate Phillips Recording, working with artists such as Johnny Cash, Bob Dylan, Phil Collins, John Prine, the Cramps, and many more.

Today the studio appears almost exactly as it did when Phillips first opened it. It's run by his family as an active recording facility with an analog focus.

PHILLIPS RECORDING STUDIO

Because it's a working studio, public tours are not available, but the building's eye-catching vintage signage is absolutely worth a look.

What: The other Phillips recording studio

Where: 639 Madison Ave.

Cost: Free to see

Pro tip: Explore the Edge District after you see Phillips Recording; there's plenty of art and things to see and do.

According to the *Memphis Press-Scimitar* in 1960, Phillips called this studio the "Cape Canaveral of the recording business" because of the advanced technology and mastering capabilities in the building.

FREE MUSIC AT THE LEVITT SHELL

Where was the first rock 'n' roll concert?

It's a warm summer evening in Memphis, and thousands of people are making their way to the sloped grassy knoll in front of the Levitt Shell amphitheater in Overton Park. The place is packed, filled with couples in lawn chairs sipping wine, families sprawled out on blankets, and friends sharing picnics and food truck grub. There's a state-of-the-art sound and lighting system, and the music, which might be a local group or a touring band, sounds amazing.

This is the scene at the Levitt Shell today, at one of its fifty free annual concerts. While it's a beloved Memphis institution now, the shell has had its ups and downs, and most people aren't familiar with the history behind this historic spot. The WPA built this amphitheater, and matching ones around the country, in 1936. It had metal bleachers and hosted symphonies and concerts. In 1954 Elvis played the first rock 'n' roll concert

THE LEVITT SHELL

What: Site of the first rock 'n' roll show

Where: 1928 Poplar Ave.

Cost: Usually free

Pro tip: Visit during the day to explore on your own or Thursdays through Sundays in spring, summer, and fall for music and crowds.

Here's a fun fact: the same architect who designed the Levitt Shell designed Graceland.

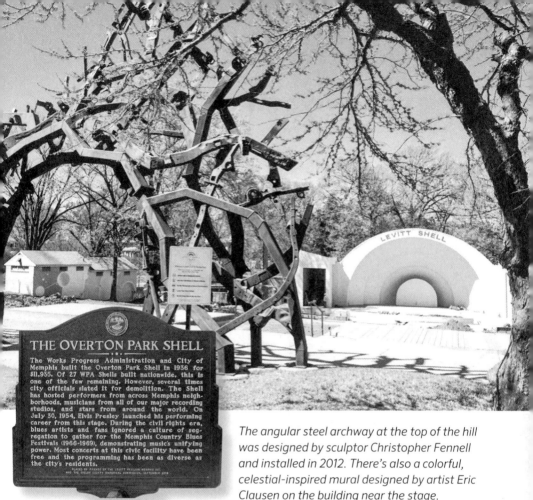

THE OVERTON PARK SHELL

The Works Progress Administration and City of Memphis built the Overton Park Shell in 1936 for $11,935. Of 27 WPA Shells built nationwide, this is one of the few remaining. However, several times city officials slated it for demolition. The Shell has hosted performers from across Memphis neighborhoods, musicians from all of our major recording studios, and stars from around the world. On July 30, 1954, Elvis Presley launched his performing career from this stage. During the civil rights era, blues artists and fans ignored a culture of segregation to gather for the Memphis Country Blues Festivals (1966-1969), demonstrating music's unifying power. Most concerts at this civic facility have been free and the programming has been as diverse as the city's residents.

PLACED BY FRIENDS OF THE LEVITT PAVILION MEMPHIS INC. AND THE SHELBY COUNTY HISTORICAL COMMISSION, SEPTEMBER 2019

The angular steel archway at the top of the hill was designed by sculptor Christopher Fennell and installed in 2012. There's also a colorful, celestial-inspired mural designed by artist Eric Clausen on the building near the stage.

there—although he was just an opening act, by all accounts he stole the show. Over the years, the amphitheater's sister shells in other cities were demolished, leaving Memphis's as one of the few still in use. From the 1960s to the 1980s there were numerous attempts to raze the shell, usually to turn the space into parking garages or commercial lots. Various groups and citizens delayed the destruction each time, and the Save Our Shell, Inc., group hosted free concerts for years with the stage's rainbow paint job in the arches. Finally, in 2005, the city formally renovated the theater and renamed it the Levitt Shell.

FIRST BAPTIST BEALE STREET

Where did Ida B. Wells start her civil rights activism?

If you keep walking east on Beale Street, past the bars and dance halls, you'll find a bright white, Gothic-inspired church. The significant history of the First Baptist Beale Street Church is unknown to most people who walk by on their way to and from the party district. First Baptist Beale Street Church was the South's first brick place of worship built by African Americans for African Americans after the end of slavery in the 1860s. Two presidents, Ulysses S. Grant and Theodore Roosevelt, have spoken at the church. In 1892 it was home to the *Memphis Free Speech* newspaper, a paper serving the city's African American community owned by journalist and civil rights activist Ida B. Wells. Though her time in Memphis was short-lived, the city made a permanent mark on Wells's career and on the nation's civil rights struggles.

FIRST BAPTIST BEALE STREET

What: First brick church built for and by African Americans in the Mid-South

Where: 379 Beale St.

How much: Free

Pro tip: A few blocks away, you can see the Ida B. Wells historical marker at 211 Beale Street, part of the Memphis Women's Legacy Trail.

The church is still operational for weekly services, which is your only chance to see inside.

Stop at the significant location, always unnoticed by the crowds enjoying Memphis nightlife on Beale, or plan to attend a service.

That same year, Wells published a story about the lynching of three wrongfully accused, untried black businessmen. Her journalistic efforts to expose the truths of segregation and lynchings in the South angered some white Memphians, and they marched down to First Baptist on Beale Street. They broke into the church and destroyed the paper's printing presses, which resulted in Wells's departure from the city. These events influenced the rest of her life, which she dedicated to antilynching activism, investigative journalism, and cofounding organizations such as the NAACP and civic clubs for African American women. The church still holds weekly services, but it is closed to the public during the week.

ST. JUDE'S HIDDEN GARDEN

Who is buried at the gold dome at St. Jude?

You've certainly heard of St. Jude Children's Research Hospital, named for the patron saint of hopeless causes, but many people don't realize that this incredible place is located in Memphis. Founded by second-generation Lebanese-American Danny Thomas and his wife, Rose Marie, the hospital's mission is to provide lifesaving cures for childhood cancers and other illnesses that threaten children around the world. Danny was a successful and popular television actor and performer for nearly fifty years, and his dream to provide a place where "no child would die in the dawn of life" came to fruition when St. Jude's doors opened in 1962. At the time survival rates for childhood cancers hovered around 20 percent; today, the survival rate has surpassed 80 percent. When Danny and Rose Marie passed away, hospital officials created the garden as a special place on campus to honor their work and St. Jude's lifesaving mission.

Hospital tours should be scheduled separately, but visitors in good health are welcome to visit the Danny and Rose Marie Thomas Memorial Garden on St. Jude's campus. The garden itself is a unique feat of natural design, home to twenty

It's stunning to think about, but no family ever receives a bill for their treatment at St. Jude. The hospital is mostly funded by generous donors from around the world.

In 2019 St. Jude was certified as a Level 2 Arboretum by the Tennessee Urban Forestry Council, extending the garden's urban tree canopy and diverse tree species to the entire campus.

DANNY AND ROSE MARIE THOMAS MEMORIAL GARDEN

What: A hidden hospital garden

Where: 262 Danny Thomas Pl.

Cost: Free

Pro tip: Check in with St. Jude security on your way to visit the Memorial Garden.

species of trees, including one of only two white oaks living in Tennessee (planted by St. Jude nuns sixty years ago) and a tree that Thomas brought from his family's home nation of Lebanon and planted there. Adjacent to the garden is the Thomases' crypt and the striking gold dome of the ALSAC Pavilion.

It's a peaceful place, built to shield visitors, patients, physicians, and St. Jude employees from the noise of downtown. If you go, take a moment to acknowledge decades of scientific research, outstanding patient care, and the generosity of supporters who make it all happen.

ELVIS'S MEMPHIAN THEATER

Where can I sit in Elvis's favorite movie theater seat?

It's the mid-1960s and you're a huge Elvis fan living in Memphis. Lucky for you, the King still spends plenty of time in his home city, and though he's normally tucked away at Graceland, he goes out on the town from time to time. If you wanted your own Elvis sighting, you could try to get a coveted invite to one of his all-night movie parties at the Memphian Theater. He'd watch the flicks on repeat all night long, allowing only a few fans in at a time to sit in the back of the theater while he and Priscilla sat up front.

Today this building still has its retro facade and vintage charm, but it's home to the Circuit Playhouse, part of the Overton Square entertainment district. See a show or take a Memphian Theater Elvis Tour. The tours are by reservation only and are most popular during Elvis Week in August and his birthday celebration in January, which shows that only the most diehard fans know about it. And you can forget an Elvis mug or keychain, because the Circuit Playhouse has one-of-a-kind souvenirs such as original Memphian Theater seats, movie ticket stubs, and other rare items.

Experience dramas, musicals, and more at the Circuit Playhouse and its sister theater across the street, Playhouse on the Square.

24

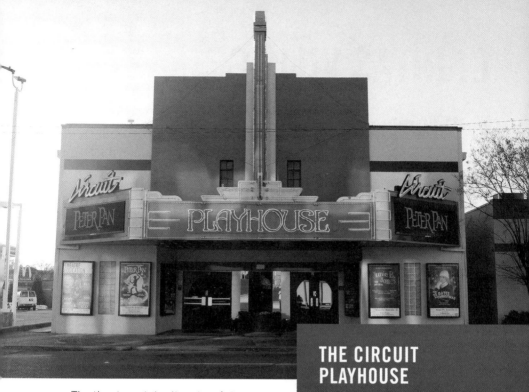

The theater retains its retro, Art Deco-inspired facade and neon lighting.

THE CIRCUIT PLAYHOUSE

What: Former site of Elvis's favorite movie theater

Where: 51 S. Cooper St.

Price: Tours are $5 per person

Pro tip: Call or email ahead of time to reserve your tour.

On the tour, you'll hear about how Elvis often rented out the entire theater to watch Hollywood's latest releases, picked up from the Memphis Film Exchange before the public had a chance to watch the movies. Today, you can see his exact seat and learn more about his favorite flicks, then come back later to watch a musical or dramatic production. Your fellow theatergoers will have no idea they're sitting where Elvis sat.

CARITAS VILLAGE

What's up with a "village" that serves lunch?

It's Wednesday at lunchtime in a clean but no-frills building in the Binghampton neighborhood in Memphis. The space is a café with booths along the windows, tables spread across the room, and a commercial kitchen and counter space on one side. On any given day you're likely to see a decent crowd of locals—businesspeople on lunch break, neighborhood residents, families with kids—but this safe haven is more unknown than known in the city. Which is a shame, because the kitchen puts out a delicious menu of home cooking and farm-to-table dishes inspired by upscale restaurants.

CARITAS VILLAGE

What: A community café with farm-to-table fare

Where: 2509 Harvard Ave.

Price: Under $10

Pro tip: Try the daily special and add a few bucks extra to your bill for someone who needs it.

Memphian Onie Johns founded Caritas Village in 2000, when she served community meals and hosted meetups at her home. In 2006 Caritas opened in a former Masonic lodge with a coffeehouse, community gathering place, and café. No one is turned away for their inability to pay for a meal. Today you can visit the space and try dishes such as pork tenderloin with maple glaze and coq au vin with handmade pasta, plus plenty of soups, sandwiches, and salads. The daily special comes highly recommended, and if you have a little extra in your wallet, you can always pay it forward.

Caritas Village is in a former Masonic lodge building.

Caritas also hosts meetings, performances, film screenings, and other community events.

TIGERS AROUND TOWN

Why are there tiger statues everywhere?

If you are for some reason looking for tigers in Memphis, you're in luck. There are one hundred of them spread out all around the city, hanging out in front of barbecue joints, set up in front of banks and hospitals, and lurking around university campuses. Of course, tigers are not native to Memphis, at least not strictly in the zoological sense. They're the mascot for the University of Memphis, and these near-life-size statues of the big cats were installed in 2012 during the school's centennial year by the Alumni Association.

Each one is painted or decorated in a unique way by an artist. The majority are painted in colorful flowers and patterns, or in a semirealistic manner, orange with black stripes. There are quite a few, however, that show off the city's quirky, artistic side. One is painted to look like it's wearing a sparkly Elvis jumpsuit, and another is covered in shards of mirrored glass. Several have interpretations of classic paintings, such as *The Scream*

UNIVERSITY OF MEMPHIS MASCOTS

What: Colorful tiger statues around town

Where: Various locations

Price: Free

Pro tip: A quick Google for *Tigers around Town* will produce a map.

Even though plenty of the tigers seem to have similar inspirations (sports, tiger stripes, flowers), no two are exactly alike.

This tiger at the Memphis Botanic Garden was dedicated by the Class of 1958 in honor of A. Duncan Williams. Left: This tiger at the Memphis Botanic Garden was dedicated by the Class of 1958 in honor of local businessman A. Duncan Williams.

and *The Starry Night*. One tiger statue pays homage to Memphis's namesake city with Egyptian emblems and designs, and another is decoupaged with superhero comic pages. Then there's the one inexplicably painted to look like the Blue Power Ranger.

If you want to see the *Tigers around Town* statues, you'll have to do some searching online. The group of one hundred were only together on the University of Memphis campus for one year before being dispersed around the metro area.

IT'S 2 A.M. AND WE'RE AT ALEX'S

Where can you eat the best ribs, wings, and burgers all in one place?

Have you ever been to a place that feels like it's existed forever? Alex's Tavern seems like it opened before the dawn of time, each booth and barstool permanently fixed to the earth and the space around it. The truth is that Alex's Tavern didn't open until 1953, and owner Rocky Kasaftes has worked there his whole life.

Inside the dim bar you'll find plenty of TVs broadcasting local sports, a vintage shuffleboard table, and an ancient but functioning analog jukebox. Order a pitcher of beer and settle into a place that still feels like a secret even when every table is full. Still, the average visitor won't make it a point to sidle up to Alex's well-worn bar and ask for a rack of Rocky's ribs at midnight. Which is exactly what you should do. (If that's too late for you, the place technically opens in the late afternoon.)

Memphis is first and foremost a BBQ town, with

ALEX'S TAVERN

What: Sixty-six-year-old tavern with a killer food menu

Where: 1445 Jackson Ave.

Price: Varies

Pro tip: Alex's is cash only, though there's an ATM inside.

If the BBQ, burgers, and wings are not enough, Rocky has been known to make a mean gumbo too.

Neon signs and a sign beckon thirsty patrons to Alex's day and night. Inset: The analog jukebox plays the classics. Photo courtesy of Alex's Tavern.

hot wings coming in second for the city's signature dish. Half the bars in town claim to make the best burger around too. Rocky's claim to fame is that he does all three, and does them well. There's the Greek burger, with hand-formed, seasoned patties, cooked in the tiny kitchen; then there are the limited quantities of barbecued ribs, smoked out back and considered by some to be the best in town. The chicken drummies are beloved by many a wing aficionado as well. Alex's is a dive bar's dive bar, but the place has layers.

MEET MARY THE GHOST

Is the Orpheum Theatre haunted?

Today the Orpheum Theatre downtown is well known as an elegant specimen of glamorous days gone by. Outside, the bright modern marquee flashes the latest Broadway show or concert to come through town. Inside, lush crimson carpeting, gilded fixtures, and sparkling chandeliers take you back in time. While the Orpheum is famous for its beauty and theatrical offerings, the playhouse has a strange history, hidden from most theatergoers. In fact, this place may be one of the most haunted spots in Memphis.

While reports of ghosts have rolled in steadily for sixty years, the most famous phantom is that of a young girl named Mary. She died in the 1920s, either in the fire that burned the theater to the ground or in a tragic trolley car accident on the street. Strange but mostly harmless occurrences have been reported, and several claim to have seen the little girl running through the halls.

ORPHEUM THEATRE

What: A beautiful, haunted theater

Where: 203 S. Main St.

Price: Show costs vary; $10 for reserved tours

Pro tip: The theater offers private tours for groups of twenty or more when scheduled ahead of time.

Mary seems to have claimed a certain seat in the balcony, C-5, so the Orpheum leaves that seat open during shows.

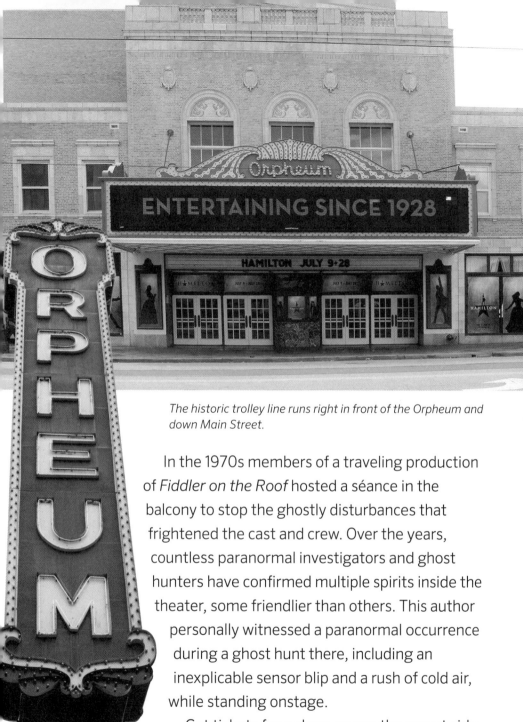

The historic trolley line runs right in front of the Orpheum and down Main Street.

In the 1970s members of a traveling production of *Fiddler on the Roof* hosted a séance in the balcony to stop the ghostly disturbances that frightened the cast and crew. Over the years, countless paranormal investigators and ghost hunters have confirmed multiple spirits inside the theater, some friendlier than others. This author personally witnessed a paranormal occurrence during a ghost hunt there, including an inexplicable sensor blip and a rush of cold air, while standing onstage.

Get tickets for a show, or see the secret side of the Orpheum during public tours on select Mondays throughout the year.

BASS PRO PYRAMID

Why on earth does Memphis have a giant pyramid?

If you've been to Memphis, you know that we have a giant glass pyramid. It's hard to miss, towering more than three hundred feet above the Mississippi River in the heart of downtown. What you may not know is: why did someone build this pyramid, and what's inside?

The original Memphis was a city on the Nile River in Egypt. European explorers made the connection between that African city's geography and the riverside bluffs they observed in the place in the New World they named Memphis. For many years, this is where the connection to the Egyptian namesake and the Tennessee town ended.

Then, in the 1990s, the City of Memphis and Shelby County built the "Great American Pyramid," an arena for Memphis Tigers basketball, the NBA's Grizzlies, concerts, and events. The arena was active for about thirteen years. After a decade of vacancy, the outdoors megaretailer Bass

BASS PRO PYRAMID

What: A giant glass pyramid

Where: 1 Bass Pro Dr.

Price: Free to enter, $10 to ride to the top of the elevator

Pro tip: Take the elevator at dusk to watch the sun set over the Mississippi River.

Embrace the weirdness of a modern-day pyramid and enjoy the unmatched view from the top.

Questions for
Sally

address ~
7794 King College Ave
Apt 207 Germantown, Tn 38138
* Memphis Light Gas
AT&T
+ Water

welcome letter

/ cable
< electric hookup)
who do we call?

_____

Moving — is moving
available on Saturday

Do you have a moving list of
requirements

online rent payment

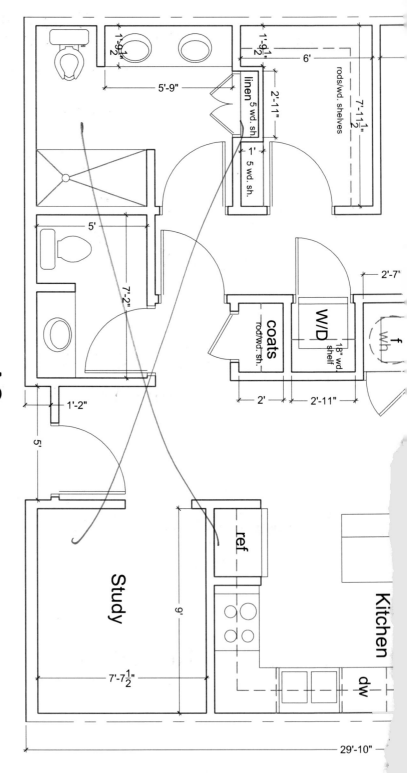

A2

linen 5 wd. sh

5 wd. sh.

rods/wd. shelves

7'-11½"

6'

1'-9½"

1'-9½"

2'-11"

1'

5'-9"

5'

7'-2"

1'-2"

5'

coats rod/wd. sh.

W/D 18" wd. shelf

2'-7'

wh. f

2'

2'-11"

Study

ref

Kitchen

dw

9'

7'-7½"

29'-10"

The main entrance of the Pyramid, facing the south side.
Left: *The nation's tallest freestanding elevator takes you to the Lookout restaurant on the top of the Pyramid.*

Pro Shops renovated and reopened the Memphis Pyramid in 2015, complete with an enormous neon-green fish logo.

Exploring the Pyramid today is a surreal but worthwhile experience. There is a cypress "swamp" complete with floating boats and live alligators, a full-size bowling alley, an archery range, a luxury hotel, the nation's tallest freestanding elevator, and enough taxidermy for a natural history museum.

HIDDEN JADE MUSEUM

Where is the "Jade Museum" in Memphis?

In a basement on Main Street in downtown Memphis, there is a twenty-four-thousand-square-foot treasure trove. Inside the Belz Museum of Asian & Judaic Art, you'll discover a dazzling array of carved jade, ivory sculptures, ancient Chinese artifacts, and artworks from generations of Jewish painters and sculptors. The place feels a bit random, situated between the Blind Bear speakeasy and the Center for Southern Folklore, and while the museum is clearly marked, something about its setup makes it easy to miss if you're not looking for it.

But missing this place would be a mistake. With more than fourteen hundred items collected over the years by locals Jack and Marilyn Belz, the museum opened in 1998 with a focus on the Qing Dynasty, China's last, which ended in 1911 after a 260-year reign. In 2004 the Belz Museum opened a Judaica gallery with art and sculpture from Jewish artists and a Holocaust Memorial Gallery.

If you visit, you can see life-sized sculptures of animals, including the Monkey King (a Chinese literary character), a three-foot-tall royal ship carved out of jade, and endless shelves of vases, figurines, and, the most fascinating of all, Chinese puzzle balls.

THE BELZ MUSEUM

What: Impressive collection of Asian and Jewish art

Where: 119 S. Main St.

Cost: Adults, $6; students, $4; children under 5, free

Pro tip: The Belz Museum is closed on Mondays.

It took skilled artisans decades to carve intricate, interlocking designs into delicate spheres of ivory, and you can see many examples at the Belz.

The eclectic exhibits at the Belz Museum contain one of the largest collections of nineteenth-century Chinese art in the world.

PIONEER SPRINGS TRAIL

Is there a real natural spring in the woods?

Set along the Mississippi River, Meeman-Shelby Forest State Park offers plenty of hiking, biking, and horseback trails. The park is a bit of a secret itself, with most of the trails nestled in a thick forest about twenty minutes north of downtown Memphis. One of the trails, Pioneer Springs, is a four-mile path through the dense forest at the base of the Chickasaw Bluff. About one and a half miles in, you can visit the trail's namesake, a real, flowing spring. You'll hear the soft sound of gurgling water, and then you'll see the spring itself.

Before the area became a state park in the 1930s, it was farmland and homesteading land for plenty of families who were likely supplied water by this spring and others like it. Today, Pioneer Springs is contained within a concrete basin and has a basic shelter and wooden footbridge nearby. If you decide to go exploring in Shelby Forest on this trail or the others, expect to see plenty of wildlife and a lush forest, including cottonwood, sycamore, oak, bald cypress, tulip poplar, and beech trees. While the spring looks clear and refreshing, it's best to bring your own water.

SHELBY FOREST

What: A natural spring in the forest

Where: 910 Riddick Rd., Millington

Cost: Free

Pro tip: As with any trail, be sure you check conditions before you go.

Poplar Tree Lake at Shelby Forest is fun for paddleboarding and fishing, but a fishing permit is required. Left: *Trails lead through heavily wooded areas on the Chickasaw Bluff at Shelby Forest.*

After a day at the park, you'll want to stop into the Shelby Forest General Store for grilled burgers and any other provisions you might need.

CRYSTAL SHRINE GROTTO

Does Memphis have any caves?

How can a place that has its own guest book—filled with signatures and notes written by people from around the world—still feel like a solemn, private escape? The Crystal Shrine Grotto at Memorial Park manages to do just that. The man-made cave sits in the middle of the sprawling East Memphis cemetery and was created by Mexican artist Dionicio Rodriguez in the 1930s and '40s. He was hired by Memorial Park to build several installations in the cemetery, including water features and Annie Laurie's Wishing Chair, but the best known is the Grotto.

It took Rodriguez eight years to construct the above-ground cave with faux-finished concrete that resembles boulders and wood; he covered the interior walls completely with crystals and the ceiling with quartz formed like small stalactites. It's dim and trippy inside, especially with the moody lighting shining on the numerous sculptures and dioramas that depict scenes from the life of Christ. The figures are more than a little haunting. There might be soft music piped in from somewhere to add to the psychedelic feel, or it might be oddly quiet, but it's certainly a memorable place.

> **CRYSTAL SHRINE GROTTO**
>
> **What:** A man-made cave filled with sparkles and sculptures
>
> **Where:** 5668 Poplar Ave.
>
> **Cost:** Free
>
> **Pro tip:** Don't forget to sign the guest book.

Reflecting pool near the Crystal Shrine Grotto.
Left: The Abraham's Oak part of the grotto, in front of the Crystal Shrine entrance.

No one's actually buried under or in the cave, but it's still best to be respectful when you visit.

MID-SOUTH COLISEUM

Is the Liberty Bell hidden inside the coliseum?

It's only been closed since 2006, but the Mid-South Coliseum is already a legendary place for Memphians who remember its heyday. The mystery is: what's inside now, and what will happen to this venue? The coliseum hosted everyone and everything, from Elvis, the Rolling Stones, and the Beatles to plenty of basketball and Andy Kaufman and Jerry Lawler's famously "brutal" wrestling match.

The coliseum opened in 1964 as the premier arena in Memphis and was one of the first to be racially integrated. It's chock-full of secrets and forgotten history, like when the Beatles stopped in Memphis in '66 in the wake of John Lennon's comments comparing the band's popularity to that of Jesus. They hosted a contentious press conference in a room at the coliseum. Anti-Beatles sentiment was high in the religious South, and Memphis city leaders even made an official proclamation that the band was unwelcome in town. The huge crowds showed otherwise.

The venue faced demolition in the 2010s, but citizen group Coliseum Coalition formed in 2015 to save the building. It has hosted cleanups and numerous tours of the interior, which

---

The coliseum hosted plenty of Memphis pro sports teams, including the Wings and RiverKings in hockey, the soccer-playing Rogues, and the Pros, Tams, and Sounds, all of the American Basketball Association.

The domed Coliseum sits at the Fairgrounds, next to Liberty Bowl Memorial Stadium.

MID-SOUTH COLISEUM

What: Historic venue slated for renovation

Where: 996 Early Maxwell Blvd.

Cost: Free

Pro tip: Follow Coliseum Coalition on social media for opportunities to tour the building or attend events.

revealed the potential for revitalization as well as plenty of interesting items, such as a replica Liberty Bell from the dismantled Libertyland theme park nearby. While the future of the Mid-South Coliseum is still being determined, the city has committed to saving and adapting the building for reuse, so you may be able to see inside its storied concourses for yourself one day soon.

CHISCA HOTEL

How did Elvis first get on the radio?

Everyone knows about Elvis sites such as Graceland and Sun Studio in Memphis, but most people don't realize that one of the most significant events in rock 'n' roll history happened in a historic hotel on Main Street that rarely gets recognition for its role in Elvis's career.

In 1954, Dewey Phillips was an incredibly popular radio disc jockey, broadcasting his nightly show *Red, Hot, and Blue*—a program that featured both black and white music—on WHBQ. His one hundred thousand listeners enjoyed the mix of jazz, country, and rhythm and blues music that he played live from the mezzanine level of the Chisca. Dewey was a friend of Sam Phillips of Sun Records, who sent Dewey a few cuts of a young Elvis Presley singing the old R&B tune "That's All Right, Mama." On July 10, 1954, Dewey played the album live during his show six times in a row and called Presley on the phone to come downtown to the Chisca *right then* for a live interview.

From the 1970s to the 1990s, the Chisca served as headquarters to the Church of God in Christ, but it fell into disrepair, becoming an eight-story eyesore on Main Street.

The Chisca building is now home to apartments and restaurants.

Happy times were ahead, though, and the hotel reopened as luxury apartments and restaurants in 2016. Though plenty of historic and original elements remain in the Chisca's architecture, there aren't any signs of the radio station or Elvis's moment there. You'll just have to meditate on the rock history that happened above your head while you dine at the popular Catherine and Mary's restaurant on the ground level.

The Broadway musical *Memphis* is loosely based on the life of DJ Dewey Phillips.

THE PEABODY'S SECRET ROOM

Did Elvis ever stay in the Peabody Hotel?

Step off the beaten path—and around the crowds waiting for the delightful Duck March—and find yourself in a secret room tucked inside the beloved historic hotel in downtown Memphis. The Peabody Hotel is glamorous in a way that feels historic, but never dated. Originally opened in 1869, the current structure was built in 1925 and went through its ups and downs, just like downtown Memphis as a whole. Businessman Jack Belz reopened the Peabody in 1981, and the hotel became a guiding force in downtown's revitalization. It's full of secrets and pieces of history, but you can discover them if you know where to look.

The memorabilia room, located on the mezzanine level

PEABODY HOTEL'S MEMORABILIA ROOM

What: A secret room full of history

Where: 118 S. Second St.

Price: Free to visit; hotel tours, $10

Pro tip: The paid tour is well worth it for entertainment and historic value; be sure to make reservations.

The Duck March tradition started in the 1930s, when the manager at the time set his live duck-hunting decoys loose to frolic in the fountain as a joke.

The Peabody is designed in an Italian Renaissance Revival style.

of the Peabody, contains significant historic documents and information you won't find anywhere else. In the northwestern corner of the level, you'll find a well-appointed mahogany room lined in glass cases filled with artifacts, letters, and photos from the hotel's 150 years of history. You can get the backstory on the ducks, of course, but a lesser-known Peabody treasure is a contract, typed on Peabody letterhead, dated November 21, 1955, and signed by Elvis Presley himself. It was on that day that Elvis's manager, Colonel Tom Parker, signed the young singer to a contract with RCA Records at a meeting at the Peabody. While it's unsure if Elvis ever actually spent the night in the hotel, he certainly experienced one of the most significant moments of his career in the lobby there.

THE MAN IN BLACK

Where did Johnny Cash play his first show?

Steps away from the bustling Cooper-Young neighborhood's eponymous intersection stands a man in black, holding a guitar. In June 2019 this statue, dedicated to American music legend Johnny Cash, was unveiled and dedicated to the music history of the area. The sculptor is Memphis filmmaker and artist Mike McCarthy, who led the nonprofit group Legacy Memphis in its mission to install the statue and adjacent historical marker.

Though Cash was born in Arkansas, he was living in Memphis in 1954 when he was first signed to Sun Records and began to release country singles. His first public performance was with guitarist Luther Perkins and bassist Marshall Grant (the "Tennessee Two") in December of that year at Galloway United Methodist Church, which is the building next door to the statue. The church has been used most recently as a music and event venue and is frequently the setting for music videos and photography. It was also featured in the CMT series *Sun Records*, where it stood in for the black church where Elvis found musical inspiration.

The statue was funded by more than 150 donors, including fans from Switzerland, Germany, and Finland, as well as plenty of local businesses and residents.

48

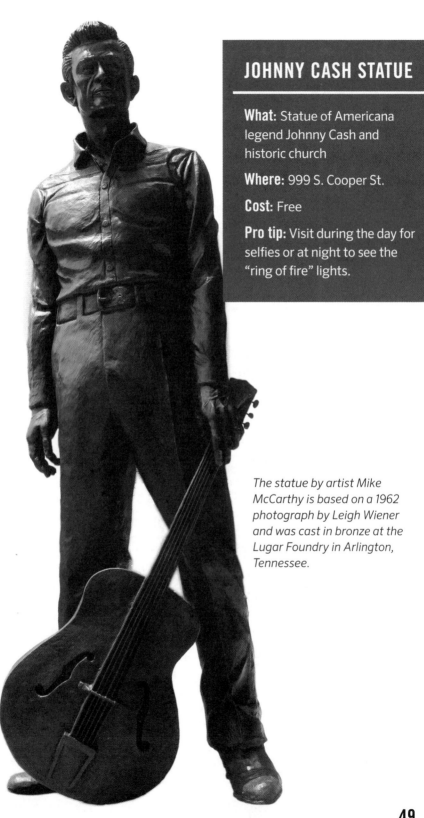

JOHNNY CASH STATUE

What: Statue of Americana legend Johnny Cash and historic church

Where: 999 S. Cooper St.

Cost: Free

Pro tip: Visit during the day for selfies or at night to see the "ring of fire" lights.

The statue by artist Mike McCarthy is based on a 1962 photograph by Leigh Wiener and was cast in bronze at the Lugar Foundry in Arlington, Tennessee.

LUCKY HEART COSMETICS

What's the story behind the "Lucky Heart" mural downtown?

On the side of 409 South Main Street, there's a simple mural that states "Lucky Heart Thank You for Our Blessings" with an understated red shamrock emblem. It's a frequent backdrop for engagement and wedding photos, and a stop for art tours in the district. It's also a clue to the history of one of the oldest African American beauty supply manufacturers in the country.

Lucky Heart Cosmetics was founded in Memphis by Jewish chemist Morris Shapiro to produce hair and skincare products targeted for black consumers. Because African Americans were not allowed to shop in department stores, Lucky Heart developed a network of representatives à la Avon to call upon families in

LUCKY HEART COSMETICS

What: Historic black beauty company still in business

Where: 409 S. Main St. (mural); 939 Dr. Martin Luther King Jr. Blvd. (shop and mural)

Price: Varies

Pro tip: If you like the mural at the original Lucky Heart location on Main, keep exploring the area—there are tons of murals nearby.

There's another mural at the current shop, a colorful piece featuring the Memphis skyline, the pyramid, and a Lucky Heart heart.

The side of 409 South Main, the original Lucky Heart location.

rural areas across Tennessee, Mississippi, and the rest of the South. Lucky Heart has long since moved from its location at 409 South Main, but it has another mural and storefront at its manufacturing facility on Dr. Martin Luther King Jr. Boulevard a few miles away.

At the store, you can shop for shampoos, creams, and colognes made on site, and you can take a look at some of the vintage Lucky Heart products and advertisements on display inside. You can also shop online, and there are still sales reps who sell products by phone to longtime loyal customers.

SILKY'S IRISH DIVING GOATS

Are there really goats on Beale Street, or did I drink too many Divers?

It's Saturday night on Beale, and Silky O'Sullivan's Irish bar is hopping. In one room, tourists and locals make requests for the dueling piano players on stage. On the sprawling patio, neon palm trees light up tables filled with young people drinking out of big yellow buckets. As for the palm trees, no one seems to care that the plants are native to neither Memphis nor Ireland; as for the buckets, they're filled to the brim with a ruby red concoction called a Diver.

SILKY O'SULLIVAN'S

What: A bar with lucky goats on the patio

Where: 183 Beale St.

Cost: Silky's Divers are $21 and serve multiple people.

Pro tip: Don't worry, the goats don't actually dive.

We could talk about the Diver recipe, which is a carefully guarded but much-discussed Memphis secret that most people agree involves beer, vodka, and grenadine. But the real curiosity is the fenced-in treehouse area on the patio, with a sign that warns, "Beware! Irish Diving Goats!" The bar is truly home to two lucky lady goats. The original owner, Silky Sullivan, started the tradition of hosting goats in the bar, inspired by the Irish belief that goats are lucky. Several generations of goats have lived in Silky's over

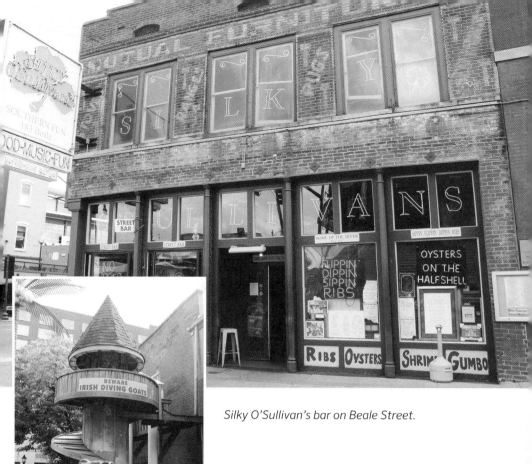

Silky O'Sullivan's bar on Beale Street.

the years, including one named Maynard who became famous for his proclivity for chugging beer and bestowing luck on the Grizzlies in the early 2000s. Fans paraded Maynard around the Pyramid before Grizz games and threw shamrocks. The team won, and Maynard then toured the country providing luck (or not) to teams and arenas in New Orleans and Chicago. Since Maynard passed away, the goat house has been occupied by friendly female goats who are less into beer and sports and more into chilling on the patio.

53

METAL MUSEUM GATES

Who made the rosettes on the Metal Museum gates?

The Metal Museum is the only one of its kind dedicated to fine metalwork, with a working foundry on site, a sculpture garden, and a blacksmith apprenticeship program. Since 1979, the campus, comprising historic buildings that were once a part of the hospital next door, has been open to the public.

On the tenth anniversary of the museum's opening, a set of sixteen-foot-tall, fifteen-foot-wide forged steel gates, with scrollwork details, gold leaf, and more than 330 decorative rosettes created by an international cohort of metalsmiths, was installed at the entrance. These miniature sculptures vary wildly in style, subject matter, and material. It seems like each time you visit, you find a new one to marvel at.

Many of the rosettes are inspired by flora, including flowers, plants, and literal rosettes. Plenty more are abstract shapes or symbols; some appear polished and gilded, while others are rough-hewn with patina. There are

THE METAL MUSEUM

What: Ornamental gates at a unique metalworking facility

Where: 374 Metal Museum Dr.

Cost: Free to see the gates; $6 to enter museum

Pro tip: Don't skip the blacksmithing demonstration at the smithy.

The museum features rotating and permanent exhibits and lovely grounds, and it also hosts plenty of workshops and community arts events on campus.

Gates leading to the museum spaces, foundry, and sculpture garden.
Inset: *Close-up of a few of the gate's rosettes.*

plenty of animals as well—a cartoonish snail reaching from its shell, a smirking wolf, a growling bear—and at least a few human faces. Some of the artists pay homage to human industry, portraying a sailing ship, a cup-bearing hand, and, of course, an anvil.

It's easy to walk through the hulking metal gates of the museum and appreciate them as you pass by; however, not enough people stop and take a look at the individual ornaments that decorate each row of the black iron gates. If you're interested in learning more, the museum gift shop offers an entire book dedicated to the rosettes.

THE WONDER OF THE WOLF

Where is the best kayaking in Memphis?

You can see what the Memphis area looked like centuries ago, and it's not a diorama in a museum exhibit or grainy photo— it's your view while floating down the Wolf River. The Wolf River is a spring-fed tributary of the Mississippi that's about one hundred miles long, reaching through West Tennessee and North Mississippi.

A trip in a canoe or kayak down the Wolf offers an ecological variety show, through tree-lined channels, wetlands, bald cypress swamps, and peaceful lakes. While a handful of locals enjoy the river regularly, most don't realize the incredible beauty of this waterway right under our noses, preserved almost exactly as it was hundreds of years ago.

How did such a huge swath of land survive development for all these years? Thank the Wolf River Conservancy, founded in 1985 to stop a gravel mine construction project that threatened one section of the river. To date, the conservancy has protected sixteen thousand acres of riverside land, including the two most popular sections: the Ghost River and the Lost Swamp.

The conservancy offers guided tours on the first Saturday of each month. Visit wolfriver.org for more info on boat rental and instructions.

The vibrant autumn leaves create a beautiful setting for kayaking the Wolf River.

THE WOLF RIVER

What: A protected river running through the Mid-South

Where: 100+ miles through Tennessee and North Mississippi

Cost: Varies

Pro tip: If you've never kayaked before, check out Shelby Farms Park's Hyde Lake first.

Despite their ominous names, these sections are more peaceful than haunting. You'll paddle past the mossy knees of towering cypress trees and navigate through swamps teeming with wildlife. Signs direct paddlers through the winding waterways, but it's always best to go with a group or hire a guide.

BOTANIC GARDEN BROOD

Why is there a flock of chickens in the botanic garden?

When you think of botanic gardens, you likely think of manicured paths through tidy collections of flowering plants, shrubberies pruned into uniform shapes, flowing fountains, lily-filled ponds, and lush groves of trees. The Memphis Botanic Garden does offer all of this, and as you stroll through the gardens, listening to the birds chirp and the soft breeze rustle through the trees, you'll forget you're in the city. Then you'll hear the rooster crow.

The garden's ninety-six acres contain more than thirty specialty gardens, including the original arboretum, a fanciful playground, a Japanese garden with a bright red bridge spanning a koi pond, and . . . a chicken house. Most visitors have no idea that the Botanic Garden raises chickens as a part of its Urban Home Garden, which, in addition to a chicken

The fanciful playground, My Big Backyard, includes plenty of creative play space for kids, including a castle made of reclaimed materials and a giant treehouse.

The chicken coop at the Botanic Garden.
Inset: *One of the blue buff Columbian Brahma hens that lives at the gardens.*

house, also has an edible garden, outdoor cooking demo area, and composting space.

The fully functional chicken coop is home to a brood of blue buff Columbian Brahma hens and their rather vocal rooster. They lay eggs for eating and hatching adorable chicks, and they do all the pecking and poking around that you'd expect a bunch of backyard chickens to do—you just probably didn't expect them to be doing it in the middle of the botanic gardens.

BIRTHPLACE OF A LEGEND

Where was Aretha Franklin born?

Before Aretha Franklin made her mark on the music universe via her Detroit-based Motown soul, she was born in a humble shotgun house in South Memphis in 1942. Her father, Reverend C. L. Franklin, was a Baptist minister in Memphis before moving his family to Detroit when Aretha was a toddler.

Though her family lived in the house for only a short time, the now-abandoned home still attracts dedicated music fans and sightseers looking for photo ops off the beaten path.

While there is a historic marker on site that details Ms. Franklin's early life, there is not much else on the property to note the music legend's time there. In 2012 the uninhabited house suffered fire damage, and the building was narrowly saved from demolition in 2016. The home now sits boarded up, and plans for its future are currently uncertain.

After Franklin's death in 2018, crowds of people arrived at the house to pay their respects with flowers and signs, and held a candlelight vigil. There was renewed talk of turning the home, which still supposedly has some original fixtures, into a

To see another famous birthplace that has been turned into a useful community space, check out the home of legendary blues singer and pianist Memphis Slim adjacent to the Stax Museum of American Soul Music.

Handmade signs adorn the chain-link fence outside the home.

ARETHA FRANKLIN'S BIRTHPLACE

What: Birthplace of Aretha Franklin

Where: 406 Lucy Ave.

Cost: Free, but donations may be accepted

Pro tip: The home is on private property (though empty) in a quiet neighborhood, so keep your visit brief and stay on the street for views and photos.

small museum or even moving the home to another area of town for restoration and usage. While it remains to be seen what will happen at 406 Lucy Avenue, you can still stop by to pay your respects to the Queen of Soul's Memphis roots.

LEGACY OF GEORGIA TANN

Who was Georgia Tann?

From the 1920s through the 1940s, a Memphis woman named Georgia Tann operated the Tennessee Children's Home Society, an "adoption agency" that popularized adoption for wealthy families during a time when such matters were secretive. She was viewed as a model citizen, someone who helped orphans and young mothers unable to care for their babies find homes with wealthy families and Hollywood celebrities. But there was a dark, tragic side to her work.

Just days before Tann's death in 1950, a state investigation discovered that many of the adoptive children were actually stolen or kidnapped, or their parents had been tricked by Tann into believing their babies

---

TENNESSEE CHILDREN'S HOME SOCIETY MONUMENT

What: Memorial for nineteen kidnapped children

Where: Elmwood Cemetery, 824 S. Dudley St.

Cost: Free, but donations are accepted

Pro tip: The cemetery accepts donations to maintain its grounds and important markers like these.

Professional wrestler Ric Flair was one of the children whom Georgia Tann placed through her black-market adoptions.

The monument honors nineteen of the Tennessee Children's Home Society victims.

had died at childbirth. She then turned around and forged birth certificates and sold these children in out-of-state private adoptions for exorbitant fees. An unknown number of children also died due to neglect while in the care of Tann's organization.

While this is a dark chapter in Memphis history we'd rather forget, the result was reform in the adoptive agency community. The story of Georgia Tann and her victims has been immortalized in dozens of television shows, books, and podcasts. In 2015 Elmwood Cemetery raised the money to provide a headstone to honor the victims of her negligence.

A DARING RESCUE

Who was Tom Lee, anyway?

It's the first weekend in May, and downtown Memphis is absolutely packed with excited people. Music fans fill Tom Lee Park for Memphis in May's first annual event of the year: the Beale Street Music Festival. Thousands of people, four stages, an electric crowd energy, and lots of corn dogs and beer are probably too distracting, and most festivalgoers don't take note of the statue on the northern side of the park. But on quieter days, the striking piece stands out.

The statue depicts a man in a small lifeboat, reaching out to a second man who is splayed on his back, clutching a piece of broken wood; curls of bronze indicate that they're both in the water. The scene is from the 1925 sinking of the *M. E. Norman*, a steamship that carried hundreds of engineers and their families visiting Memphis for a convention. History says that the steamer capsized, and a man on a small boat nearby rushed to the passengers' aid, selflessly rescuing thirty-two people. That man was Tom Lee, a black river worker who became a hero for his bravery in rescuing a boat full of white people who lived a very different life from him.

After his death in the 1950s, the city erected an obelisk a few yards north of the current statue with a problematic inscription that called Lee "A Worthy Negro." Perhaps nature

---

There are thirty-two lights in the plaza around the Tom Lee statue, which is the number of people he rescued.

TOM LEE PARK

What: Monument honoring the namesake of a downtown park

Where: Riverside Drive

Cost: Free

Pro tip: Visit Tom Lee Park at dusk for a stunning view of the river and sunset over the Mississippi.

The monument sits on the banks of the Mississippi River.

also took issue with the racism of the marker: the obelisk is gone after windstorms cracked and toppled it in 2003 and again in 2017.

In 2006 the UrbanArt Commission and sculptor David Alan Clark worked in collaboration with Lee's descendants to erect the current Tom Lee Memorial.

TAKE A PICTURE WITH LITTLE MILTON

Who's sitting on the bench at the Blues Hall of Fame?

If you're walking down South Main and you see a refined older gentleman perched on a bench—and not budging—with a guitar in front of the Blues Hall of Fame, feel free to sit on down and take a selfie with him.

The life-size bronze statue pays tribute to the late blues musician Little Milton Campbell, a Mississippi Delta native who was inducted into the Hall of Fame in 1988. He had multiple chart-topping hits in the 1960s and worked with Memphis labels such as Stax and Sun. The statue itself was sculpted by Andrea Holmes Lugar and cast in bronze by her husband, Larry Lugar. The bench was created by artists from the Metal Museum and is called a "gar bench" because the shape of the legs is reminiscent of the shape of a gar fish.

BLUES HALL OF FAME

What: Bluesman statue in front of the Hall of Fame

Where: 421 S. Main St.

Cost: Adults, $10; students with ID, $8; children 12 and under, free

Pro tip: The National Civil Rights Museum is directly across the street. Grab a trolley ride and tour the entire area, which is chock-full of the weird and wonderful.

If you're a true fan of the blues, set aside plenty of time to spend inside the museum. It has thousands of tracks available for listening on headphones in sound booths.

THE BLUES FOUNDATION

The Blues Foundation, the world's premier organization dedicated to honoring, preserving, and promoting the blues, was founded in Memphis in 1980. Mississippi-born performers and business professionals in the Foundation's Blues Hall of Fame outnumber those from any other state, and Mississippians have also won many annual Blues Music Awards, Keeping the Blues Alive Awards, and International Blues Challenge talent competitions sponsored by the Foundation.

A marker installed by the Mississippi Blues Commission explains the mission of the Blues Foundation. Inset: Bronze sculpture of blues musician known as Little Milton.

The Blues Hall of Fame building opened to the public in 2015, a few months after the statue was unveiled during a ceremony attended by Little Milton's widow, Pat Campbell, and other friends and colleagues. Inside the museum, you'll find hundreds of artifacts from blues musicians, songwriters, and music executives who contributed to the form of music born and bred in the Delta surrounding Memphis.

The Blues Hall of Fame was started in 1980 by the Memphis-based Blues Foundation, an organization that continues to support the blues of the past, present, and future. Every year, it hosts the International Blues Challenge on Beale Street, which brings in hundreds of blues performers from around the world for a music showcase and competition.

A GRAND CAROUSEL

What ever happened to the rides at Libertyland?

When the carousel struck up its tinny tunage for the first time in years in 2017, it was no secret to Memphians who'd grown up enjoying the ride at the Fairgrounds. But the Grand Carousel, now at the Children's Museum of Memphis, has a history full of twists and unexpected turns, from its creation to years in hiding to its current glory.

The only thing most Memphians know about the carousel is that it was at Libertyland, the city's Americana-themed amusement park open from 1976 to 2006. Before then, the ride had been a staple at the Fairgrounds since 1923 and was added to the National Register of Historic Places in 1980. The carousel was originally built in 1909 in Philadelphia at the workshop of renowned carousel creator Gustav Dentzel.

After Libertyland theme park hosted its last star-spangled summer, the carousel and all the rides—including the Zippin Pippin wooden roller coaster—were stored in the nearby Mid-South Coliseum for nearly a decade. In 2015 the Children's Museum of Memphis leased the carousel from the city and sent it off in pieces for a $1 million restoration. The spectacular merry-go-round, featuring carefully restored all-original wood carvings and fixtures, reopened in its own special pavilion in December 2017. There are forty-eight unique horses, plus two chariots, including one that is ADA-accessible.

Elvis was known to rent out the entire park at Libertyland, and it's said his favorite horse is the one decked out in Native American-inspired accessories.

The Grand Carousel was painstakingly restored over several years.

As for the rest of the Libertyland rides, most of them were sold off or tossed out. The Zippin Pippin roller coaster, made famous by Elvis's affinity for the ride, was sold to the city of Green Bay, Wisconsin, where it is still offering rides at Bay Beach Amusement Park.

TUNE IN TO DɪᴛᴛyTV

Is Memphis home to a secret international music channel?

There's an international TV station broadcasting to millions from the heart of downtown Memphis, and hundreds of people walk by it every day without even knowing it's there.

DittyTV is a streaming service dedicated to Americana and roots music such as folk, blues, rock, country, gospel, and more. The station broadcasts twenty-four hours a day, seven days a week with a full program of music videos, concert tapings, and recorded hosted shows such as *Stand By Your Van*, featuring music and videos inspired by touring, and *Soul Side*, which focuses on the soul subgenre of Americana. Amy and Ronnie Wright founded their online streaming station in 2012 and had dedicated it fully to Americana and roots music by 2014.

DittyTV also broadcasts performances, many of which are recorded live in its studio space. The venue's location, unknown to most Memphians (or anyone), is kept under lock and key, but if you get an invite inside, you'll be transported to a cozy, lively dreamland lit in purples, blues, and pinks, filled with memorabilia and art. Artists such as John Oates, Ray Wylie Hubbard, Robert Randolph, and Kevin Bacon's band, the Bacon Brothers, have played for a handful of lucky

---

DittyTV is supported by the Ditty Foundation, a nonprofit dedicated to promoting modern American and roots music.

Exterior window of the Vibe & Dime shop on Main Street.

listeners—and thousands more viewing via smart TVs and online streaming services.

In 2019 DittyTV opened a retail shop next door to its studio called Vibe & Dime, where you can shop for music, gifts, and Ditty merch. While the storefront isn't as clandestine as the studio next door, you can still get a feel for what the station is broadcasting to millions from the other side of the wall.

DittyTV HEADQUARTERS

What: A secret TV studio broadcasting Americana music

Where: 510 S. Main St. or online

Cost: Free; donations accepted

Pro tip: You can stream DittyTV directly from dittytv.com, from any kind of smart TV, or from your mobile device.

THE BLUE HOUSE ON BEALE STREET

Who lives in the little cottage on Beale Street?

If you're strolling down Beale during the day or come to the east end of the street while you're enjoying the music, crowds, and drinks at night, you may be surprised to see a charming blue cottage surrounded by a white picket fence, tucked back away from the street next to a police station. As interesting as it could be to reside in one of America's most famous entertainment districts, no one actually lives inside the house anymore.

The aging little house on Beale belonged to the "Father of the Blues," W. C. Handy, and was originally located at 659 Jennette Place in South Memphis. In the 1980s it was moved to Beale Street and served as a modest museum and interpretive center. Despite being on Beale, the house is still set off from the main drag sufficiently enough to be practically hidden.

The two-room shotgun house looks as out of place on the street as you'd expect; it's a standalone residential structure in the shadow of the FedExForum arena and AutoZone Park ballpark, a few doors down from clubs, bars, and concert venues. The curious setting makes the W. C. Handy house worth a stop.

"Father Of The Blues"

W. C. HANDY HOUSE

What: Former home of the Father of the Blues

Where: 352 Beale St.

Cost: Free to see; tour costs vary

Pro tip: Contact Heritage Tours for information on a guided tour of the home.

W. C. Handy is also honored in the eponymous park on Beale Street, and you can see additional artifacts from his life and work at sites such as the Blues Hall of Fame and the Memphis Music Hall of Fame.

MEMPHIS BUFFALOES

Why are there buffalo in a city park?

If you know where to go, you can find a herd of buffalo roaming at their leisure within Memphis city limits, and it's not at the zoo. Shelby Farms Park is a forty-five-hundred-acre recreation destination (five times the size of New York City's Central Park) that boasts miles of trails, multiple lakes, and plenty of things to do, from disc golf to horseback riding to boating and biking.

It's been a public park since the 1970s, and since 1989 it's also been home to a small herd of American bison. The park started out with just six animals as part of the national effort to restore the native buffalo population, and people loved them so much, the park embraced it. Today the herd number varies depending on how many calves are born each year, but it's usually about fifteen animals.

As of 2013, the buffalo have a fifty-acre pasture designed just for them, with plenty of native grasses to eat, lots of shade, and a self-filling water trough. The park rangers stay busy caring for the animals, who drink about thirty gallons of water per day.

People often ask why the pasture fence is so high, as it seems excessive for buffalo. Turns out, these massive animals

---

Before its days as a public park, Shelby Farms Park was a penal farm where residents grew award-winning produce and built one of the area's first underground grain silos (where Hyde Lake is now).

Buffalo at Shelby Farms. Photo courtesy of Shelby Farms Park.

SHELBY FARMS PARK BUFFALO HERD

What: Buffalo roaming in an urban park

Where: 6903 Great View Dr. N.

Cost: Free

Pro tip: If you want to see buffalo calves, your best chance is in April and May.

are not always as docile and peaceful as they seem— buffalo are surprisingly athletic for their shape and size, and they can actually leap up to six feet high. While it's rare to see a one-thousand-pound animal hit that six-foot vertical, Shelby Farms Park isn't taking any chances and keeps the fence at eight feet for everyone's comfort and safety.

BEFORE GRACELAND

Did Elvis always live at Graceland?

It may not have a jungle room, and it may not have a series of Hallmark holiday movies based on its charms, but Lauderdale Courts is still an essential stop on a deep-dive Elvis tour around Memphis.

Elvis moved here with his parents Vernon and Gladys from Tupelo, Mississippi, in 1949. Lauderdale Courts was one of the first housing projects in the country designed for lower-income families; in fact, there was a limit on household income, which is why the Presleys eventually had to leave. But for about four years, young Elvis built his community and gathered his influences from the neighborhood. The housing project's communal spaces provided Elvis with places to informally perform or practice for his neighbors and friends. The home was near Beale Street's music clubs, the Poplar Tunes record shop, and Humes High School, where he attended.

LAUDERDALE COURTS

What: Elvis's first home in Memphis

Where: 252 N. Lauderdale St.

Cost: Call ahead for prices

Pro tip: You're near plenty of Memphis landmarks at Lauderdale Courts, including the Renasant Convention Center, the Bass Pro Pyramid, and St. Jude Children's Research Hospital.

Lauderdale Historic Homes is a designated spot on the Memphis Heritage Trail.

LAUDERDALE COURTS

Built in 1936 by the Federal Emergency Administration of Public Works, Lauderdale Courts was one of the first federal housing projects in the nation. It replaced substandard housing with clean, modern dwellings for the poor. The Courts were built along property adjoining Bayou Gayoso, which had been lined in concrete and covered by the extension of Lauderdale Street. Designed in the Georgian Revival style, the Courts contained 449 apartments in buildings one to three stories high. Part of Market Street was converted to green space. Memphis Housing Authority (MHA) selected families based upon financial need. Conforming to the segregation laws of the time, only white families were considered for residency. In 2000, MHA renovated the Courts into mixed-income housing under the Hope VI program and renamed it as Uptown Square.

A historical marker is your only clue that Elvis used to live here.

Local history preservationists, business leaders, and Elvis fans saved Lauderdale Courts from demolition in the 1990s. These days, it's called Uptown Square, and all the rooms have been remodeled, except the former Presley family residence. That apartment, 32B, is designed to appear as it did during Elvis's adolescence, right down to family portraits, clothing, movie posters, and documents such as paystubs and ID cards. You can stop by the outside or call ahead to schedule a tour of the interior.

ROCK 'N' SOUL MUSEUM

Is there a Smithsonian museum in Memphis?

While other museums and music history sites in Memphis mostly focus on one genre of music or a particular artist, the Memphis Rock 'n' Soul Museum takes the Smithsonian commitment to primary sources and multimedia and tells the full story of Memphis music. The museum places in context the music of Memphis with the people who made the music, from sharecroppers in the fields of the Delta to jazz and blues on Beale, from soul and R&B to rock and hip-hop at Memphis studios in recent decades.

MEMPHIS ROCK 'N' SOUL MUSEUM

What: Music museum with social context

Where: 191 Beale St.

Cost: Adults, $13; children 5–17, $10; children 4 and under, free

Pro tip: This museum is a stop on the free shuttle that also goes to Sun Studio and Graceland.

The Memphis Rock 'n' Soul Museum began as a traveling Smithsonian Institution exhibit called *Rock 'n' Soul: Social Crossroads,* which was aimed at sharing the story of roots music born in the Southern Delta, and found its permanent home on Beale Street in 2000. It was the first museum created as a collaboration between a local group and the Smithsonian Institution.

The Memphis Rock 'n' Soul Museum sits in the shadow of FedExForum and is filled to the brim with artifacts, photos, and audio clips that let you see and hear the experience. There are multiple jukeboxes throughout the building so you can actually hear what the exhibits describe.

The Memphis Rock 'n' Soul Museum displays
a neon sign from Orange Mound, the first
community in the country built for and by
African Americans after the Civil War.

THE HOUSE OF MEWS

How many cats are in there?

How much is that kitty in the window? Folks strolling down Cooper Street in Midtown are often surprised to stumble upon a storefront full of snoozing cats. The House of Mews is on the main drag in Cooper-Young, but it's set back barely a hair from the street with an overhang. It wouldn't stand out at all if not for the colorful baskets containing dozens of cats who hang out in the large display windows.

The House of Mews is a cat rescue that's achieved low-key landmark status in the neighborhood, partly because of people's natural curiosity and partly because of its longevity. The rescue began in 1994 with the volunteer work of Elain Harvey, who cared for cats on the location of Goodwin's Nursery in Germantown, a suburb of Memphis. In 1995 the cat rescue (called "Puddy Tat Protectors, Inc." according to its nonprofit designation) went to the Cooper-Young neighborhood, and in 2007 it moved to its current storefront.

One of the most common questions heard from

THE HOUSE OF MEWS

What: A free-range cat rescue

Where: 933 S. Cooper St.

Cost: Free

Pro tip: If you enjoy the visual of dozens of happy kitties, drop a donation inside or make one online.

All of the cats are spayed or neutered, and none of them are "for sale," but donations from adoptive cat parents keep the rescue running.

passersby is, "How many cats are in there?" The House of Mews reports that at any one time, about sixty cats have free roam of the store, and the newer cats and kittens who haven't been adopted yet spend their first few months in cozy kennels until they've acclimated to the environment. They're cared for by a dedicated staff of volunteers.

You can tell that House of Mews is still a fairly well-kept secret by the reactions of the people who walk by, do a double take, and turn back to peer through the windows with surprise. Some of the cats will interact with visitors through the glass, some are too busy snoozing, and others are, naturally, keen to completely ignore all humans.

CHICKASAW MOUNDS

Who built the giant hills by the river?

No place holds as many clues to Memphis history as Chickasaw Heritage Park. At this site just south of downtown Memphis, you can climb prehistoric Native American mounds, see where Hernando de Soto first viewed the Mississippi River in 1541, and look for the remnants of Fort Pickering from the Civil War.

Paleo-Indians inhabited the region for thousands of years before Europeans arrived. They established villages and built ceremonial earthen mounds like the ones at Chickasaw Heritage Park and the nearby Chucalissa Archeological Site. When Spanish colonizer Hernando de Soto brought his troops through the area, they encountered the Chickasaw people, who were using the mounds as a fortress for their chief, Chisca.

The Chickasaw lived in the Mid-South until the 1830s, though by then European settlers had forced them to a smaller territory in north Mississippi. At that time, the US government forcibly removed the Chickasaw and four other Southern Native American tribes through an arduous, deadly relocation journey known as the Trail of Tears. There are two Trail of Tears informational markers in Memphis: one at Tom Lee Park and another at Greenbelt Park on Mud Island.

For more Native American history, explore the grounds and exhibits at the C. H. Nash Museum at Chucalissa. It's just 15 minutes away from Chickasaw Heritage Park.

CHICKASAW HERITAGE PARK

What: Native American ceremonial mounds

Where: Metal Museum Drive

Cost: Free

Pro tip: Take care climbing up and down the mounds.

During the Civil War, the Confederate Army built Fort Pickering on the bluff, digging bunkers into the mounds; the fort was captured by the Union Army and used for weapons storage. Today, these prehistoric man-made hills are surprisingly steep and amazingly intact. They rise from the banks of the river and provide some of the best views in the city.

The *Legacies* statue at the park was created by artist Vinnie Bagwell in 2010. It depicts a Chickasaw woman as the primary figure, with other images carved in relief, including an African woman and child, a Spanish explorer, and an African American guitarist. It's a part of the Memphis Women's Legacy Trail.

SEX PISTOLS TACO BELL

Where did the Sex Pistols play in Memphis?

You may need some imagination and humor to appreciate this tidbit of Memphis history, but if you want, you can make a pilgrimage to the site of the Sex Pistols' one and only Memphis show on January 6, 1978. The only problem is, it's now a Taco Bell.

In the 1970s this site on Union Avenue was a deteriorating venue called the Taliesyn Ballroom, which was attached to the Nineteenth Century Club. You can get an idea of what it was once like by checking out Red Fish, a Japanese restaurant now inside that historic, upscale club. By the time British punk rockers the Sex Pistols arrived in Memphis, however, the Taliesyn had seen better days. At the last minute before the show, the fire marshal reduced the number of people allowed inside.

The show was already sold out, which meant that an angry group of a few hundred cold and locked-out Memphians reportedly threw rocks and made some noise, but ultimately kept it together. Inside, Johnny Rotten, Steve Jones, Paul Cook, and Sid Vicious (whose chest was visibly sliced up with self-inflicted wounds) performed a forty-five-minute set that included "God Save the Queen" and "Pretty Vacant."

The Memphis concert was the second of only seven shows that the Sex Pistols played on their only tour of the United States.

Unassuming but busy, the Sex Pistols Taco Bell serves Midtowners all day and night.

SEX PISTOLS TACO BELL

What: Where the Sex Pistols played

Where: 1447 Union Ave.

Cost: Free

Pro tip: See how many tacos you can buy with $3.50, the cost of the 1978 show ticket.

A year later, Sid Vicious died of a heroin overdose and, unrelatedly, the Taliesyn Ballroom was torn down. The Sex Pistols show influenced a generation of Memphis musicians and arguably kick-started the city's punk scene centered around the Antenna club. Years later, a Taco Bell was built on the site of the Taliesyn. In 2013, that Taco Bell was demolished and replaced by a newer Taco Bell, destined to forever be known as "the Sex Pistols Taco Bell."

SILKY'S IRISH DIVING GOATS (PAGE 52)

LADY LIBERTY, MEMPHIS EDITION (PAGE 154)

BASS PRO PYRAMID (PAGE 34)

Artwork by Kyle Taylor

REVIVING THE MEMPHIS SPIRIT (PAGE 146)

THE LABYRINTH BY THE TREE OF LIFE (PAGE 12)

ONE-STOP CULTURAL SHOP (PAGE 172)

EXPLORE THE CROSSTOWN CONCOURSE (PAGE 130)

ROCK 'N' SOUL MUSEUM (PAGE 78)

HOTEL PEABODY

November 21, 1955

Received of Colonel Tom Parker the amount
of forty five hundred dollars ($4500) for
the following:

RCA VICTOR BONUS
($5000 less 25% $1250)........$3750.00

WILL AND JULIE
($1000 less 75% $250)........... 750.00

TOTAL TO ELVIS PRESLEY $4500.00

This amount received by ELVIS PRESLEY
on November 21, 1955.

*RCA Victor Bonus — 5000.00
Due to contract dated
Nov 15 1955 (as per Nov 21 1955
Paragraph 4 (A)

Contract donated by
Norm Seifert

RCA recording contract signing at The Peabody.
Nov. 21, 1955
Left to right: Jim Crudgington, Colonel Tom Parker, Elvis Presley,
Hank Snow, Bob Neal, H. Coleman Tily, III & Sam Esgro

Elvis Presley's RCA Signing Bonus

THE PEABODY'S SECRET ROOM (PAGE 46)

THE WONDER OF THE WOLF (PAGE 56)

SECRETS OF RHODES COLLEGE (PAGE 114)

TUNE IN TO DittyTV (PAGE 70)

CHICKASAW MOUNDS (PAGE 82)

CLAYBORN TEMPLE

What happened at the Clayborn Temple?

Clayborn Temple began its service as the Second Presbyterian Church in 1883, when it was one of the largest churches in the Southeast. In 1949 the African Methodist Episcopal Church purchased the building and renamed it Clayborn Temple. In the 1960s the building became a meeting place for the civil rights movement in the South, under the leadership of Reverend Benjamin Booker. In 1968, during the Sanitation Workers' Strike, Clayborn Temple was used as a distribution hub for the iconic "I AM A MAN" signs and a stepping-off point for the march, the cause that attracted Dr. Martin Luther King Jr. to the city.

Let's take a look at a few other significant sites in Memphis, though. The Lorraine Motel was rebuilt as the internationally known National Civil Rights Museum in 1991, and the Mason

CLAYBORN TEMPLE

What: Historic church and civil rights landmark

Where: 294 Hernando St.

Cost: Free

Pro tip: If you visit the site near lunchtime, hop around the corner for a meal at Lunchbox Eats, a cute cafeteria-inspired café with hearty Southern dishes.

The adjacent plaza, designed by Cliff Garten Studio, in collaboration with Memphis poet Steve Fox, features an original poem engraved in marble along with the names of the thirteen hundred people who took part in the 1968 Sanitation Workers' Strike.

Left: *The Clayborn Temple building is under renovations.* Below: *The I AM A MAN sculpture reflects the light in the evening.*

Temple was an active church building before and after King gave his final "I've Been to the Mountaintop" speech in 1968. In contrast to these well-known civil rights sites in Memphis, the Clayborn Temple slowly fell into disrepair, forgotten and vacant even as the multimillion-dollar FedExForum arena opened next door in 2004.

Today the temple is in the process of restoration. As part of the fiftieth anniversary of King's assassination in 2018, a memorial plaza was installed adjacent to the building. The site is a part of the Memphis Heritage Trail.

Its unique Romanesque Revival architecture, bell tower, and stained-glass windows earned the building a spot on the National Register of Historic Places in the 1970s; in 2017 the church's listing was updated to include its role in the civil rights movement and its current name.

MEET ELMER AT THE DIXON

Where's the oldest tree in Memphis?

After exploring the formal gardens of the Dixon Gallery & Gardens, keep walking toward the eastern edge of the property. You'll see a towering elm tree presiding over bright cerulean moss, branches reaching across the entire clearing, the huge trunk buttressed by roots.

The tree, affectionately known by Dixon staff as "Elmer," is one of the oldest and largest elm trees in the city. It's impossible to say whether it's the oldest, because its actual age is unknown. We know that it was already on the grounds when Hugo and Margaret Dixon built their home in 1941, and Dixon horticulturists are confident that it's at least one hundred years old.

The stately elm grew in the backyard of the Dixons' Georgian estate for many years, but Elmer had already been through a lot before they moved onto the property. In the 1920s and '30s, Dutch elm disease struck the United States, decimating the elm population throughout the country. Due to a lucky genetic mutation, this particular elm miraculously survived and has thrived for decades. After the Dixons' death in 1975, the property became the nonprofit garden and museum for education and public enjoyment that it is today.

These days, Elmer provides shade to a quiet moss garden, a ground cover plant perfectly suited to life under his

---

The sculpture that accompanies Elmer in the garden is called *Fleuriforme*. It's a marble figure by Swiss abstract sculptor Antoine Poncet, created in 1969 and gifted to the Dixon in 1988.

Elmer towers over the patch of mossy grass. Inset: Abstract sculpture in the garden near Elmer.

DIXON GALLERY & GARDENS

What: A historic American elm tree

Where: 4339 Park Ave.

Cost: Adults, $7; seniors 65+, $5; students 18+ with ID, $5; children ages 7–17, $3; children 6 and under, free

Pro tip: Grab lunch or a coffee at Park + Cherry, the Dixon's museum café and gift shop inside.

sun-blocking branches. The tree also receives occasional "shots" to keep it healthy and ward off any future illness.

The majestic tree has been out of the way of most visitors, as it's on the east end of the property behind the museum, so go experience this wonderfully peaceful spot while it's still relatively unknown. Since the opening of the adjacent Farnsworth Education Building in 2019, this special spot may start to be a little less secret.

HATTILOO THEATRE

Where is the Memphis Theater District?

It's a busy weekend night in Overton Square in Midtown. Outside, people fill restaurant patios, stroll down the sidewalks, and congregate in the courtyards. Inside, the Hattiloo Theatre's intimate performance space has been transformed into a Caribbean island, a Harlem neighborhood, or any one of the real or imagined universes where its theatrical productions take place.

Hattiloo was founded in 2006 by Ekundayo Bandele, who named the theater after his two daughters. He started the theater due to his own passion (he's an accomplished playwright) and a need to represent black performing arts in Memphis in a dedicated way. The theater is one of the only black repertory theaters in the country, meaning that it produces works written by or based on works by African American playwrights and composers.

Most people aren't aware of how rare and special a venue like Hattiloo really is, as a freestanding and fully dedicated space for black theater. The seasons are filled with a mix of dramatic plays and musicals, often award-winning works. Bandele's original play, *If Scrooge Was a Brother*, is a retelling of Dickens's classic *A Christmas Carol* from the perspective of

---

Overton Square is unofficially Memphis's theater district. It's home to multiple performing arts venues, including Playhouse on the Square, Circuit Playhouse, Ballet Memphis, and TheatreWorks.

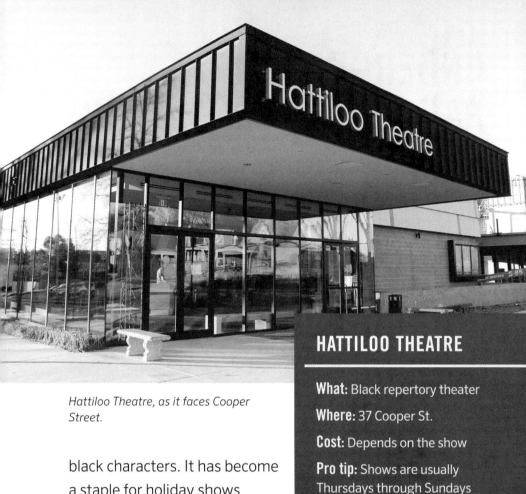

Hattiloo Theatre, as it faces Cooper Street.

HATTILOO THEATRE

What: Black repertory theater

Where: 37 Cooper St.

Cost: Depends on the show

Pro tip: Shows are usually Thursdays through Sundays and can sell out quickly.

black characters. It has become a staple for holiday shows at Hattiloo.

Other performances over the theater's fourteen seasons include beloved and well-known works such as *The Wiz, Raisin in the Sun, In the Heights,* and *Aida,* in addition to countless works by up-and-coming playwrights and regional or national premieres.

The original location for the theater was in a repurposed shop front in what we now call the Edge District; in 2014 it moved to its custom-built location in a revitalized Overton Square. Today the modern Hattiloo Theatre building contains a minimalist black box theater and space for events and education.

UNDERGROUND RAILROAD SLAVE HAVEN

Was Memphis a stop on the Underground Railroad?

Like every city, Memphis has history that we have a responsibility to remember, even if we aren't proud of these pieces of the past. The story of the Burkle Estate is one of those bits of history. In the mid-nineteenth century, Memphis was the center of the cotton trade in the United States, which also means it was a center for the slave trade.

Today an unassuming white clapboard house downtown serves as a reminder of the cruelty of this institution, but also of the power of the human spirit to stand up against that cruelty. In 1849 German immigrant Jacob Burkle built a home and a stockyard on a plot in downtown Memphis. The Burkle Estate was a convenient place for herdsmen to keep

THE BURKLE ESTATE

What: A stop on the Underground Railroad

Where: 826 N. Second St.

Cost: Adults, $12; students 4-17, college students, and seniors 65+, $11

Pro tip: Roxie's Grocery in Uptown is a one-minute drive from the Burkle Estate, and it offers the best burgers in town (for to-go orders only).

The persisting story is that the Burkle Estate was an ideal location for such a risky operation because at the time it was actually on the outskirts of town and near the thoroughfare of the river.

4E   99
BURKLE ESTATE

In the years immediately preceding the Civil War, Jacob Burkle operated the Memphis Stockyards on this site. Herdsmen seeking shelter and respite at Chelsea House found the stockyards a convenient custody station for their livestock. Folklore persists, however, that the estate was also a haven for slaves escaping to freedom on the underground railroad.

Exterior of the Burkle Estate.

their cattle, but history says that Burkle also opened his home to provide shelter and a hiding place for people who were escaping slavery via the Underground Railroad.

From 1855 until the abolition of slavery, Burkle operated this stop on the network of safe houses and routes for those making their way to the northern states and Canada. In 1997 the home and surrounding land was converted into the Slave Haven Underground Railroad Museum. This museum might be overlooked for top-ten lists, but it represents an important period of Memphis history.

The home's interior is filled with artifacts documenting the slave trade in Memphis and the experiences of those who may have passed through on their way to freedom through the Underground Railroad system.

ROYAL STUDIOS

Were "Uptown Funk" and "Let's Stay Together" recorded in the same room?

Most soul music fans have heard of Stax Records, but Stax was not the only Memphis recording studio responsible for creating the Memphis soul sound. Royal Studios and Hi Records spent the 1960s churning out R&B hits that defined an era of music for Memphis and the world.

The Royal Studios building opened in 1915 as a nickelodeon theater and spent decades as a silent movie house before being converted into the Royal Recording Studio, the home of Hi Records, in 1956. Local trumpet player Willie Mitchell joined the studio in 1963 as a session musician, eventually taking over the studio and Hi Records in the 1970s. Things picked up tremendously from there, and once Mitchell teamed up with vocalist Al Green, the pair were unstoppable. They produced some of the most popular and beloved R&B and soul hits of all time in Royal Studios, including "Tired of Being Alone," "Love and Happiness," and "Let's Stay Together."

After Willie's passing in 2010, his children Lawrence ("Boo"), Archie, and Oona Mitchell took over the family business. The studio has continued to record artists such as

---

Royal Studios looks almost exactly as it did in the 1960s, and it offers the best of both worlds in terms of recording capabilities, with modern software working smoothly with highly sought-after original analog recording equipment.

Royal Studios building in South Memphis.

John Mayer, Rod Stewart, Melissa Etheridge, My Morning Jacket, and others.

In 2014 Mark Ronson, working with pop superstar Bruno Mars, came to Royal Studios in Memphis to lay down his next album, *Uptown Special*. That album included the worldwide smash hit song "Uptown Funk," recorded in the same room as "Let's Stay Together" and countless other hits over the years. Even if you don't have a recording session, you can still go by and see the historic studio's building.

ROYAL STUDIOS

What: One of the longest-running recording studios in the country

Where: 1320 Willie Mitchell Blvd.

Cost: Free to see

Pro tip: Since Royal is one of the oldest continuously operating recording studios in the country, it's not open for public tours.

SECRETS OF RHODES COLLEGE

Why is there a school that looks like Hogwarts in Memphis?

If while traveling the tree-lined streets of North Parkway, you pass a series of towering Gothic buildings among towering oak trees, you might think you've been suddenly transported to another place and time. With its medieval-inspired architecture, buildings clad in red and brown sandstone, pointed arches, and stained-glass windows, this unexpected sight in the middle of Memphis might even remind you of a certain whimsical school for wizards.

Sadly, you won't see a quidditch game or a flock of owls descending from one of the stone towers, because it's only muggles who attend Rhodes College, a liberal arts university that opened in Memphis in 1925. The gated campus feels like a European tour destination, and it's full of curiosities such as a secret garden, hidden sculptures, messages in the library ceiling, and countless traditions that honor the school's architecture.

Students use the secluded Fisher Garden, a semihidden grass arena surrounded by a grove of trees, as a secret study spot as well as for annual commencement ceremonies. You can find limestone gargoyles perched atop walls and the faces of

Any new buildings on campus adhere to strict historical standards that maintain the magic of Rhodes. All sandstone comes from Arkansas quarries within a five-mile radius of the same spot.

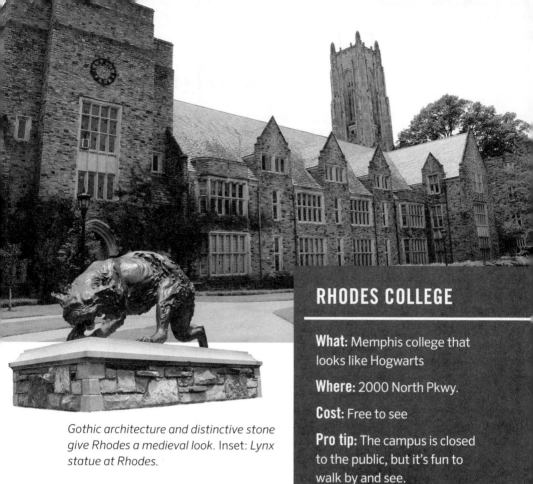

Gothic architecture and distinctive stone give Rhodes a medieval look. Inset: *Lynx statue at Rhodes.*

past Rhodes College presidents carved into the stones of the Barret Library. The stunning reading room in the library features floor-to-ceiling arched stained-glass windows and a ceiling painted with constellations in the exact configuration of the stars on the day that Rhodes opened in 1925.

Another Rhodes College secret is the senior tradition of the Pentathlon, a series of tasks involving campus landmarks. Students won't reveal the full details of the five-part quest, but we know that it involves climbing on at least two statues—touching the top of President Diehl's likeness in front of Burrow Hall and "riding" the unnecessarily terrifying sculpture of the lynx, the school's mascot—among other clandestine but harmless tasks.

THE GOODWILL STATION

What radio station is "The Heart and Soul of Memphis"?

Today Memphis radio station WDIA 1070AM plays mostly R&B and soul classics. But when this historic station started in 1948, it was the first in the United States to feature programming targeted to black listeners. The station's white owners launched WDIA with a country and pop format in 1947, but it performed poorly. In 1948 they hired African American radio personality Nat D. Williams to host his show (called *Tan Town Jubilee*), and WDIA rocketed to the number-one radio station in the city. It was the first time black Memphians heard programming that spoke to their communities and interests.

The station featured music from black musicians and all-black on-air entertainers. Legends such as B. B. King and Rufus Thomas got their starts hosting shows on WDIA that attracted major advertisers, including Lucky

WDIA HISTORIC MARKER

What: First radio station in the country targeted to black listeners

Where: 66 S. Main St.

Cost: Free to stop by

Pro tip: Today, WDIA is broadcast from an office park in southeast Memphis and still uses the tagline "The Heart and Soul of Memphis." You can listen on the radio or online.

WDIA also hired Martha Jean "The Queen" Steinberg, who was one of the first black female announcers on the radio, among many other notable DJs and personalities.

WDIA
THE GOODWILL STATION

WDIA, the Goodwill Station, was the first radio station in the nation to have an all-black format. This format made WDIA the top-rated Memphis Station in the early 1950s. In 1948, Nat D. Williams became its first black "D-J". Among those who appeared on WDIA were B. B. King, Dwight More, Rufus Thomas, A. C. Williams, Willa Monroe, Martha Jean Steinberg and Maurice Hulbert. Early programs included Teen-Town Singers, Payday Today, Brown America Speaks and Hallelujah Jubilee.

TENNESSEE HISTORICAL COMMISSION

A sign marks the spot of the original WDIA building. This location was added to the US Civil Rights Trail in 2020.

Strike cigarettes. It's said that Elvis loved the station and was influenced by the blues and gospel music he heard when he tuned in.

In the 1950s the station's wattage increased, which allowed it to reach a huge audience, stretching across the Mid-South and South through Mississippi to the Gulf Coast. It's estimated that at one time WDIA reached 10 percent of the entire African American population of the United States. The station also started the Goodwill Fund, which raised money for youth programs and children in need in Memphis's African American community.

You can visit the historical marker in downtown Memphis on Union Avenue in front of the original broadcasting building.

GARAGE ROCK PILGRIMAGE

Why is there a punk rock festival in Memphis?

When most people think of Memphis music, their brains go straight to rock 'n' roll, blues, soul, and hip-hop. But for four days every fall, Gonerfest transforms Memphis into a punk rock destination for fans of garage, grunge, metal, and whatever other "rock" music qualifiers you could imagine. There are shows at multiple venues and dive bars across town that attract an international roster of bands and fans.

The headquarters and birthplace of Gonerfest is Goner Records, which is both a music label and a real-life, yes-it-still-exists record store in the Cooper-Young neighborhood. Musician Eric Friedl started Goner Records as

---

GARAGE ROCK PILGRIMAGE

What: Memphis garage rock label and record store

Where: 2152 Young Ave.

Cost: Merchandise and ticket costs vary

Pro tip: For garage and punk shows in Memphis year-round, check out divey music- and beer-soaked venues such as the Hi Tone, Murphy's, the Lamplighter Lounge, and the P&H Café.

The cozy record shop is located in Cooper-Young and sells all kinds of local and popular music on vinyl and CD, plus Goner Records merch and memorabilia.

Inside the Goner record shop.
Left: *The Elvis Shrine inside Goner.*

an independent record label in 1993. For years, the label released music from local and international groups such as Japanese garage rockers Guitar Wolf, Canadian punk group the King Khan & BBQ Show, Jay Reatard, all-girl band NOTS, and Eric's group, the Oblivians.

In the mid-2000s, Zac Ives came on board as co-owner of the label, and the Goner name grew to include the aforementioned brick-and-mortar record shop and a punk rock festival, Gonerfest, now held every fall. Tickets for Gonerfest go on sale every summer, and the event is usually held in late September.

ALTOWN SKATE PARK

Who made the hidden skate park in Memphis?

In 2011 a group of local skateboarders found an overgrown concrete structure in Midtown and decided to take unofficial ownership, taking years to turn it into Altown Skate Park.

These days Altown is a popular skating destination featuring quarter pipes, handrails, bank walls, a vert wall, grind boxes, and more. In 2019 a crew of thirty-five to forty people, including several professional skate park builders who traveled to Memphis for the occasion, built out a "pocket" area for skating and poured two giant vert bowls, one of Altown's biggest projects yet.

But back in 2011 a dozen or so people showed up on the first day of cleanup. Armed with shovels, weed eaters, and wheelbarrows, they cleared debris, vines, and eye-high grass. They made the space more accessible, painted over layers of graffiti, and built out the access to the space, originally entered through a six-foot drop into a basin.

Organizers say they've had plenty of help from the community, holding benefit concerts to raise money for supplies and getting advice and instruction from a community of skate park DIYers from across the country. They have an

---

When *Thrasher* skateboarding magazine came through in 2014 as part of its Skate Rock music tour, it chose Altown as its venue. The huge crowd filled the space and completely drained the corner store of its beer reserves.

Brightly colored mural at Altown.

agreement with the property's owner, who is happy to let the Altown folks use the space they've worked hard to improve. They've lifted the original ban on graffiti to accommodate the park's signature street art and murals by local and visiting artists.

On the other hand, this Memphis secret may not last forever. The property is technically for sale and could meet the fate of an earlier iteration of Altown, which was demolished after that space was sold. The possible impermanence is just a part of the attitude of the secret skating spot, though, just like the murals artists spend hours creating with the understanding that another artist will eventually come along to cover it up.

ALTOWN SKATE PARK

What: Unofficial DIY skate park

Where: 849 Roland St.

Cost: Free to skate

Pro tip: There are other skate parks in town now, including Tobey Park, Memphis Skate Park, and Society Memphis's indoor skate park in Binghampton, but Altown came first.

SEE THE *BIG KIDS*

Where did these blue dudes come from?

One way to experience the Vollintine Evergreen neighborhood is to walk or run the V&E Greenline, a 1.7-mile-long unpaved trail that runs along North Parkway, through wooded areas and over creeks. If you make it to the western end of the Greenline, you'll meet three big blue people-like sculptures just hanging out on the side of the trail in various states of repose.

The official name for the sculpture is *Big Kids*, and the project was initiated by Rhodes College graduate Graham Smart as a part of his public art class in 2011. There were originally five "people" in total, each lounging along the trail in different poses, each a colorful azure hue, and each with a planter on the top of his (her?) head.

The V&E Greenline is a section of a former railroad line that served the nearby Sears distribution center, but it was abandoned in the 1980s. In 1996 the community association purchased and built out the trail, planted trees, and began volunteer-based maintenance of the Greenline. It also passes over Lick Creek via a footbridge and has a bright yellow station house on Tutwiler.

The V&E Greenline also stops near the enormous renovated Crosstown Concourse building, which is full of restaurants, shops, and art worth exploring.

The dudes are chilling in the shadow of the Crosstown Concourse.

Due to the elements, only three of the *Big Kids* remain, still as chill and content as ever. The sculptures are located on the west end of the V&E Greenline, near Stonewall Street, in the shadow of the Crosstown Concourse building.

V&E GREENLINE SCULPTURES

What: Colorful sculptures along the V&E Greenline

Where: Near Stonewall Street

Cost: Free

Pro tip: The path starts at Springdale Street and Vollintine Avenue, passes by Rhodes College, and stretches to North Watkins Street.

US MARINE HOSPITAL

What's up with this creepy abandoned hospital by the river?

Nowhere in town can beat the US Marine Hospital in terms of number of urban legends and extreme curiosity from the locals who have heard about it, or even attempted to explore it themselves over the years.

This sprawling campus is a shadow of its original stately appearance, now appearing more like a flashback from a psychological thriller, with overgrown foliage, broken windows, and huge iron fencing blocking views of the historic architecture. Photos of the interior show peeling paint, discarded medical and dental supplies, crumpling signage, a basement morgue, and other haunting images of the abandoned hospital that would not be out of place in a horror film.

The Marine Hospital opened in the 1880s, though the Georgian-style signature building with towering columns and red brick wasn't added until the 1930s. The facility served injured Mississippi River workers, seamen, Civil War soldiers, and various armed service and government employees for decades. In the hospital's early days, it was the site of scientific

---

As of 2019, plans are underway to redevelop the Marine Hospital as luxury apartments, so it may not remain a wonderfully weird Memphis secret for long.

Main building of the Marine Hospital.

US MARINE HOSPITAL

What: An abandoned, creepy hospital

Where: 360 Metal Museum Dr.

Cost: Free to peer through the iron bars

Pro tip: This location is adjacent to the Metal Museum Gates and the Chickasaw Mounds, so if you're on a hunt for Memphis secrets, it's worth it to try to find the spot.

research for the prevention of yellow fever, which plagued the city in multiple epidemics. It was last used during Desert Storm to house soldiers but generally has been vacant since 1965.

A few of the original hospital buildings are owned by the adjacent Metal Museum, which maintains the historic value of the architecture. The Marine Hospital is on the National Register of Historic Places.

THE SIX-STORY MURAL

What's the story behind the huge mural on the MLGW building?

At the intersection of Main Street and Martin Luther King Jr. Boulevard, a six-story-tall colorful mural stands out in the heart of the city. You can't miss this bright, eye-catching artwork, but many people are unaware of the stories behind the figures and vignettes that the mural depicts.

The mural, called *History of Civil Rights in Memphis*, was created in 2016 through a collaboration between artists Michael Roy and Derrick Dent, who were commissioned by the UrbanArt Commission to create the large-scale piece that reflected events with strong ties to the downtown neighborhood. Dent created sketches and initial concepts that focused on the experiences of black Memphians downtown, and the design was finalized and painted on panels by Roy, whose signature style is evident in the piece. Those panels were installed on the side of the Memphis Light, Gas, and Water parking garage downtown.

The mural sheds light on several little-known parts of Memphis history through sections that depict stylized representations of events. The top vignette shows a family in a "contraband camp," one of a group of settlements for formerly

The parade shown on the mural is specifically meant to be the Cotton Makers Jubilee, a parade celebrating the contributions of black Memphians to the cotton industry during the time of segregation.

The mural stretches six floors high on the MLGW parking garage.

HISTORY OF CIVIL RIGHTS IN MEMPHIS MURAL

What: Colorful artwork depicting civil rights history

Where: Main Street and Martin Luther King Jr. Boulevard

Cost: Free to see

Pro tip: There's plenty of cheap street parking on Main Street and side streets where you can stop and stroll through the neighborhood to check out public art and lots of the sites mentioned in this book.

enslaved black refugees from North Mississippi seeking a new life near Memphis in the 1860s. Several downtown landmarks are depicted in the towering mural, including Beale Street Baptist Church, the now-destroyed Robert Church Auditorium, a parade on Beale Street, and historic homes like those once found on nearby Mulberry Street. Other figures in the mural include black Civil War soldiers in Union army uniforms, antilynching journalist Ida B. Wells, Memphis millionaire Robert Church, and a modern-day family.

RIDE A TROLLEY

Why does Memphis have trolleys?

In Memphis, you'll find a mode of transportation that's a blast from the past: a heritage trolley system. These colorful cars clickety-clack up and down Main Street, carrying locals and tourists from the Pinch District to South Main. The interiors and seats are polished wood and the fixtures are antique, but the trolleys are temperature controlled for the modern passenger's needs.

Streetcars have been a part of Memphis transportation since the 1800s, but they were discontinued in the 1940s. In the 1990s the Memphis Area Transit Authority (MATA) decided to bring back a historic trolley line on the car-free Main Street Mall. You could ride from one end of downtown to the other for sixty cents. The fleet mostly comprised restored cars from Portugal and Australia. Two more trolley lines were added later: the Riverfront Line and the Madison Avenue Line, the latter of which led to and from downtown proper past the Medical District.

Turns out, using one-hundred-year-old trolleys for transportation comes with challenges. By 2014 the system needed safety upgrades and maintenance. All three lines

---

Check out "Trolley Night" on the last Friday of every month, when the shops in South Main host open houses, live music, gallery openings, and free refreshments all evening.

The MATA trolley fleet is powered by overhead cables and runs on tracks.

MEMPHIS TROLLEY SYSTEM

What: Historic streetcars

Where: Main Street

Cost: $1 per ride (one way)

Pro tip: You can catch a trolley about every half hour along Main Street.

were suspended as visitors and residents eagerly awaited their return. Finally, on April 30, 2018, the Main Street Line sprung back into life with a small fleet including restored W-class Melbourne trolleys and a replica Birney trolley car. There are plans in place to bring back the Riverfront and Madison Avenue lines in the future too.

Find out why people are so charmed by these antique people movers and take a ride for yourself. It's also a cheap way to get from point A to point B on Main Street.

EXPLORE THE CROSSTOWN CONCOURSE

What's inside the former Sears Crosstown building?

These days, the old Sears building on Cleveland Street goes by the name Crosstown Concourse, and it's a hub for arts, nonprofits, education, and much more. The enormous Art Deco building opened in 1927 as a major distribution center for Sears's robust mail-order catalog system.

Thousands of Memphians worked at Sears Crosstown over the decades, either in the department store or in the fulfillment center, which processed tens of thousands of orders each day. Packages were transported through the building on conveyor belts, then loaded onto the adjacent railway system and shipped to customers across the region. Over time, shopping habits changed and catalog ordering declined. In the 1990s, the building closed and remained empty for years, attracting

CROSSTOWN CONCOURSE

What: Renovated historic megabuilding

Where: 1350 Concourse Ave.

Cost: Free to enter

Pro tip: Check out the Crosstown Arts calendar at crosstownarts.org. The organization hosts events several days a week, including live music in the Green Room.

A few more fun things to find in Crosstown: pinball machines hidden around the building that anyone can play, multiple murals, and art installations.

Colorful tendrils of paper flowers flow over the staircase in the Concourse's West Atrium. Inset: *Find the ultra-cool Art Bar by climbing the neon red staircase accessible through the West Atrium.*

"explorers" and photographers who documented the decay of the cavernous space.

In 2010 the Crosstown Arts organization was formed to facilitate the rebirth of the 1.5-million-square-foot high-rise. In 2017 the LEED-certified building reopened and has become a bustling center of activity in the historic Crosstown neighborhood. While the Crosstown Concourse is clearly not a secret, most visitors (and Memphians who remember it only as an abandoned eyesore) still have no clue what's inside. If you spend a day exploring, you'll find galleries, shops, restaurants, offices, health facilities, a theater, apartments, and short-term room rentals, as well as Church Health, Crosstown High School, and a YMCA.

VIEWS AT THE RIVER GARDEN

Where can I see the bridge lights?

The River Garden is a lush downtown park on the banks of the Mississippi River, with an incredible view of the nightly Mighty Lights show on the Hernando de Soto Bridge. There's a treehouse playground, native plants and flowers, walkways, seating, and a pavilion. This park, which reopened in November 2018, provides some of the best views in town of the river, sunset, and bridge, but it is still a bit of a secret.

Before it was the River Garden at Mississippi River Park, the simple park had served downtown since the city built it in the 1930s. In 2013 the space, originally called Jefferson Davis Park, was renamed Mississippi River Park. In 2018 the Memphis River Parks Partnership and the Groundswell Design Group worked with local elementary, middle, and high school students to develop custom designs for the River Garden's play areas.

Every night, enjoy Mighty Lights, a state-of-the-art LED light show on the famous double-arched Hernando de Soto Bridge every half hour from sundown until 10 p.m. You can view Mighty Lights from the River Garden and plenty of other vantage points downtown.

The River Garden is a part of the Fourth Bluff park district, which also includes Memphis Park.

RIVER GARDEN AT MISSISSIPPI RIVER PARK

What: Picturesque park with a sunset view

Where: 51 N. Riverside Dr.

Cost: Free to enter

Pro tip: There is limited parking at the Tennessee Welcome Center adjacent to the park, but there are bike-share stations in the park and it's easy to get to by sidewalk from anywhere downtown.

The result is a system of treehouses, climbing nets, hammock swings, and hangout zones for visitors of all ages. Park goers will find occasional programming such as activities, fire pits, music, and more, plus walk-up kayak and paddleboard rentals from Kayak Memphis. Word hasn't quite gotten out about this scenic park yet, so head over for a sunset stroll, a cup of coffee, or a visit to the playground.

BLUESMAN ON BEALE

Who was W. C. Handy?

Between the blues clubs and restaurants on Beale Street, there's a park that honors the Father of the Blues, William Christopher Handy. The park, which is named after the musician, is home to a statue of his likeness wearing a sharp suit and holding his signature cornet. W. C. Handy's compositions are among the most influential in American music history, and he's credited with writing the first blues song, or at least the first commercially viable blues song, "Memphis Blues."

Handy was born in Florence, Alabama, in 1873, where he soaked up the music of the South and learned to play the cornet. He later taught music and traveled the country performing with various groups before settling in Memphis. In 1912 he published a song called "Memphis Blues," possibly based on a campaign song he wrote for longtime Memphis mayor E. H. Crump. The energetic tune became an overnight sensation, though Handy did not see profits from the sheet music sales—unfortunately, he had sold the song rights.

Learning from this experience, Handy founded his own music publishing company in 1913 and wrote more hits, including "Beale Street Blues," "St. Louis Blues," and "Yellow

---

The city opened Handy Park on Beale Street in 1930 and erected a statue of the famed composer two years after his death, in 1960.

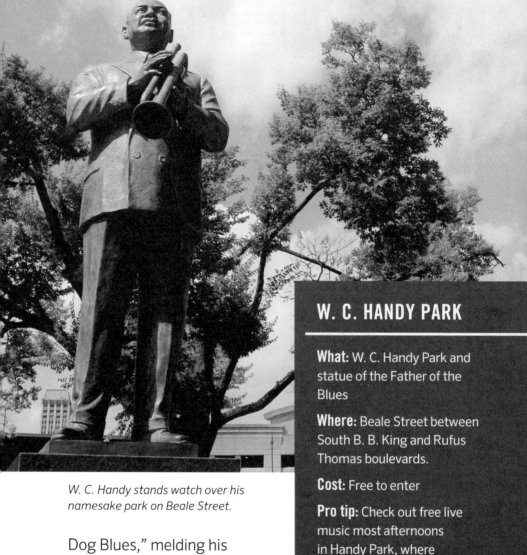

W. C. Handy stands watch over his namesake park on Beale Street.

W. C. HANDY PARK

What: W. C. Handy Park and statue of the Father of the Blues

Where: Beale Street between South B. B. King and Rufus Thomas boulevards.

Cost: Free to enter

Pro tip: Check out free live music most afternoons in Handy Park, where there's a large stage and a smaller setup for intimate performances.

Dog Blues," melding his classical musical training with ragtime, Latin rhythms, and African American music of the South to firmly establish a new genre: the blues.

BROWSE IN BURKE'S BOOKS

Is Memphis home to the oldest bookstore in the South?

Despite millions of e-book and podcast apps filling up our smartphones, the leisurely art of bookstore browsing is still alive and well in plenty of independently owned bookstores.

Opened in downtown Memphis in 1875, Burke's Books is one of the oldest, if not the oldest, bookstores in the South. The business has seen four different locations, generations of owners, the Great Depression, and the dominance of online booksellers.

Burke's can attribute its success to a gently evolving business strategy, such as opening an online shop for its enormous collection of used and rare books, and the friendly, personal experience of shopping

BURKE'S BOOKS

What: 140+-year-old bookstore

Where: 936 S. Cooper St.

Cost: Depends

Pro tip: Check the website for a schedule of author readings and book signings.

Over the years, Burke's has seen some incredibly rare books pass through its collections, including a first edition *Uncle Tom's Cabin* and a signed W. C. Handy autobiography.

Burke's has a reputation for appealing, creative storefront decorations that change seasonally.

there. The staff is happy to help with recommendations and special orders, and they're fine with you staying a while to enjoy the warm, vintage atmosphere of the shop.

The store's current owners, couple Corey and Cheryl Mesler, took over in 2000. In 2007 they moved to the present-day location, a cozy, creative space in the Cooper-Young neighborhood, a perfectly tempting shop to step into and stay a while. On the shelves, you'll find plenty of new and used books, fiction bestsellers, nonfiction tomes, Southern literature, local Memphis authors, and a young adult literature area.

A VINYL PARADISE

What's the story behind the Shangri-La Records store?

At first glance, Shangri-La Records seems like an old-school music store, the kind you still stumble across occasionally. But the place is much more than a vintage shop riding the wave of the vinyl renaissance. This hundred-year-old house's story involves sensory deprivation tanks, zines, wrestling documentaries, and a deep, deep catalog of Memphis music and local indie labels.

The story begins in 1988, when Sherman Willmott started selling music as a way to supplement his New Age-y spa concept, offering Memphians sessions in saltwater sensory deprivation tanks in the upstairs rooms. When that didn't catch on, he turned his attention to promoting music and Memphis culture in a variety of ways. In the 1990s Shangri-La became a hub for the Memphis indie scene and a source for underground tourism via Willmott's *Kreature Comforts* city guide zine. In 1999 he left the shop to curate the Stax Museum; in 2000 he founded a spinoff label,

SHANGRI-LA RECORDS

What: Thirty-year-old music shop

Where: 1916 Madison Ave.

Cost: Depends

Pro tip: The sensory deprivation tanks are long gone, but you can rent the upstairs rooms via Airbnb.

Rolling Stone named Shangri-La one of the best record stores in the country in a 2010 comprehensive national guide.

The shop hosts free live music regularly on the porch and in the front parking lot.

Shangri-La Projects, which in 2011 released the definitive documentary on Memphis wrestling, *Memphis Heat: The True Story of Memphis Wrasslin'*.

These days, Shangri-La is co-owned and run by Jared and Lori McStay and John Miller, all Memphis musicians and label owners themselves. They keep a full inventory of popular releases, promote albums from local artists and labels, and host regular live music events and discount sales such as the Purgening, Sweat Fest, and Record Store Day. They've maintained and grown Willmott's vision for supporting independent, current Memphis music.

MAKING MUSIC IN MEMPHIS

Why does Memphis have one of the largest record-making companies in the United States?

What do the Beatles, Netflix hit sci-fi series *Stranger Things*, and the Backstreet Boys have in common? All three have vinyl records produced by Memphis Record Pressing, thanks to two enterprising locals who took a chance on the record-making business back in 2014.

Before they learned the lost art of vinyl, Memphis Record Pressing co-owners Mark Yoshida and Brandon Seavers owned a media manufacturing company in the 1990s and 2000s, making CDs for music labels such as Fat Possum Records out of Oxford, Mississippi. Recognizing a need for better and faster vinyl production, the two companies partnered to create a record pressing plant just outside of Memphis in Bartlett, Tennessee.

MEMPHIS RECORD PRESSING

What: One of the four largest record manufacturing companies in the United States

Where: 3015 Brother Blvd., Bartlett

Cost: Call ahead for tour and fee information.

Pro tip: Occasionally you can find "MRP" etched in the run-off groove area of a record made at Memphis Record Pressing.

Memphis Record Pressing has pressed everything from local one-offs to major label productions, television and music soundtracks, and remastered collections.

MRP can create custom colors and styles for records, such as multicolored streaks, glitter, or neon.

This idea proved to be easier said than done. No one built record presses anymore, so the team bought salvaged presses from a shuttered plant in New Jersey. Then they had to convince engineer Donny Eastland to come out of retirement to rebuild the presses. In 2015 Memphis Record Pressing officially opened its plant. In 2016 it joined forces with GZ Media from the Czech Republic, the largest record producer in the world.

Today MRP is one of the top-four largest record manufacturers in the United States. The machines, some manual and some digital, run twenty-four hours a day several days a week, and the company employs more than one hundred people. In 2019 the company produced about four hundred thousand records per month, which means that if you've purchased vinyl recently, it's likely it came from this spot near Memphis.

CAPTAIN HARRIS HOUSE

What does a house in Cooper-Young have to do with William Faulkner?

In a neighborhood full of historic homes and colorful stories, the Captain Harris House near the corner of Cooper and Young stands out for its unique hues and architectural features, but there's much more to its history.

Painted jungle green with gold arches and rust-red trim, the Victorian home has distinctive curb appeal. You can't miss it. It was built in 1898 and purchased a few years later by one Captain C. L. Harris, whose business dealings in the railroad industry led to the Memphis home's claim to literary fame. The story goes that Captain Harris co-owned a railroad, along with his son-in-law R. J. Thurmond and a Civil War hero named Colonel William C. Falkner. The business deal went south, and Thurmond shot and killed Colonel Falkner in the town square of Ripley, Mississippi.

Falkner's public and calamitous murder only added to his mythical status, and his life and death became an inspiration for his great-grandson's writing. The great-grandson—who changed the surname spelling to Faulkner—went on to create literary legends and win the Nobel Prize in Literature.

The Captain Harris House was home to four generations of the Harris family and was used as an officer's club during

---

You could view the house from the outside, of course, or you can check out the inside by booking a room there via the affordable Airbnb rental.

The Captain Harris House is an example of American Queen Anne style architecture.

CAPTAIN HARRIS HOUSE

What: Historic home with a literary connection

Where: 2106 Young Ave.

Cost: Free to see

Pro tip: The house is just steps away from a dozen bars and restaurants, so stop in to a Cooper-Young establishment for a bite while you're there.

World War II before becoming a boarding house for the Lumbermen's Association until 1977. That's when the current owner, Chip Armstrong, moved his family in. Over the years the Armstrongs have made improvements and renovations, all while maintaining the historic character of the home and its wrap-around veranda.

LET'S DO THE TIME WARP AGAIN

Is there a drive-in movie theater in Memphis?

It's a warm April night, so you and a few friends buy movie tickets, pull your car into a sprawling lot, tune your radio, and sit back to watch an old movie at the drive-in. Have you gone back in time? No, it's just a Time Warp Drive-In night at Memphis's Malco Summer Quartet Drive-In. Time Warp Drive-In is a monthly event where moviegoers enjoy themed evenings of cult classics such as *Ferris Bueller's Day Off* and *Back to the Future*, or offbeat movies such as *Howard the Duck* and *Heavy Metal*. The movies—usually three or four of them—start at dusk and continue all night.

With only a few hundred drive-in movie theaters left in the United States, it's uncommon to find this unique movie-going experience. Luckily for Memphis, this one on our eclectic Summer Avenue, open Fridays through Sundays, is still going strong. You can catch double features of the latest superhero blockbusters, kid-friendly animated movies, or horror flicks in addition to the monthly throwback nights.

Local organizations the Black Lodge, Guerrilla Monster Films, and Holtermonster team up to present the Time Warp Drive-In nights, and you can find the monthly themes and schedule online.

On the sign:

MALCO SUMMER DRIVE IN

PROUD MARY	THE COMMUTER
12 STRONG	JUMANJI
MAZE RUNNER	PITCH PERFECT 3
TIME WARP	SATURDAY FEB 17
	OPEN FRI SAT SUN

The theater has an eye-catching sign with a yellow VW Beetle and colorful metal sculptures.

MALCO SUMMER QUARTET DRIVE-IN

What: Vintage drive-in theater with retro movie nights

Where: 5310 Summer Ave.

Cost: Adults, $7.50; Time Warp Drive-In nights, $10; kids ages 10 and under, free

Pro tip: Eat at Summer Avenue's beloved no-frills restaurants, such as Taqueria Guadalupana or Elwood's Shack, before the movie.

While movie theaters today continue to pile on amenities—plush recliners, servers bringing chicken tenders and beer to your assigned seats, high-tech surround sound—there's something charming about a night at the drive-in. For less than ten dollars, you can see two movies, and kids under ten get in for free. Not to mention that there are four screens, so moviegoers have options. The whole Summer Drive-In complex is a blast from the past, with retro mod sculptures out front and a snack bar straight out of the 1980s.

145

REVIVING THE MEMPHIS SPIRIT

What's the story behind the Old Dominick Distillery?

Back in 1859 Domenico Canale immigrated to Memphis from Italy and helped grow a thriving grocery wholesale business. A few years later, he released the first spirits from his company, a whiskey called "Old Dominick" and a flavored whiskey called a "Toddy" in a bottle emblazoned with a Dominicker rooster. Prohibition came and went, and Domenico and his descendants turned their focus to the large-scale food and beverage industry.

Four generations later, cousins Alex and Chris Canale discovered an unopened bottle of "Toddy" whiskey and were inspired to revive their family's fine spirits brand; in 2017 the Canales and their team, including head distiller Alex Castle, opened the Old Dominick Distillery in the former Memphis Machinery & Supply Co. building on Front Street.

OLD DOMINICK DISTILLERY

What: Modern distillery with Memphis history

Where: 305 S. Front St.

Cost: $12 for a tour; includes a tasting and guidebook

Pro tip: The distillery's shop is more than your average souvenir trap; it offers upscale merchandise and limited edition spirits, too.

Old Dominick is located directly across the street from the flagship location of Gus's World Famous Fried Chicken, considered a Memphis must-eat.

The distillery hosts events on the top floor, which features an interior bar and a rooftop patio. Inset: A portrait of Domenico Canale holding the company mascot, a Dominicker rooster, presides over the tasting room.

The restored industrial building gleams with polished wood, beautiful lighting, and distilling equipment that is as beautiful as it is functional. There's a large square bar downstairs for tastings, an upstairs lounge, and a rooftop bar with a view of downtown Memphis and the Hernando de Soto Bridge.

As of this writing, most of Old Dominick's whiskey is quietly ruminating in white oak barrels onsite, waiting to reach maturity. In the meantime, you can sample the distillery's vodkas, the Memphis Toddy (based on the original Canale recipe), and the Huling Station Bourbon. Take a behind-the-scenes tour and enjoy a tasting at the end, or order a drink made with Old Dominick spirits from a local watering hole.

MARTYRS PARK

Is there a hidden park along the Mississippi River?

Away from the bustle and noise of downtown, Martyrs Park is spacious and secluded, offering impressive views of the Mississippi River and the Harahan Bridge. Martyrs Park gets its name from one of the most devastating events in Memphis history, a moment so catastrophic that it's memorialized in multiple locations around town: the 1878 yellow fever epidemic. While the majority of Memphians fled the city at that time, some twenty thousand stayed, and at least five thousand succumbed to the illness. "Martyr" here references the citizens who risked their lives to stay behind and care for the sick, then succumbed to the illness themselves.

The park's centerpiece is an eerie sculpture by Harris Sorrelle. It portrays skeletal figures suspended between two columns, floating—maybe to heaven, maybe along the river. The park itself isn't as morose as the story behind its title: it's a pleasant, nine-acre, grassy bluff, dotted with magnolia trees, offering vistas of the river, bridges, and the downtown skyline.

It's easy to stumble upon the park on foot because it's at the southern end of the Riverwalk trail. On the other hand, finding Martyrs Park by car requires you to know where you're going: take Channel 3 Drive and then the road north of the television station. While you're in the area, head over to Big River Crossing, a one-mile-long pedestrian bridge just south of Martyrs Park that connects Memphis with Arkansas.

The monument, created by Memphis artist Harris Sorrelle, was installed in 1971.

MARTYRS PARK

What: A riverside park off the beaten path

Where: Channel 3 Drive

Cost: Free

Pro tip: The park is perfect for a sunset picnic or viewing the Mighty Lights nightly bridge display.

The Riverwalk is a marked pathway that runs through Martyrs Park and connects it to Ashburn-Coppock Park to the north and Tom Lee Park north of that.

BEALE STREET LANDING

Can you still ride a riverboat in Memphis?

While it may look like a man-made bluff or an ultramodern glass building set into a hill, Beale Street Landing is actually a functioning, state-of-the-art boat docking structure. It serves a busy schedule of riverboats year-round, just as Memphis has for more than 250 years.

Opened in 2014 in the space between the historic cobblestone landing and Tom Lee Park, Beale Street Landing is at the western terminus of Beale Street. There's a floating dock, a boarding ramp, an event space, a small splash park, a row of rocking chairs along the river, and a multicolored tower that looks like a construction of LEGOs.

If you're looking for a boat ride, Memphis Riverboats offers scenic and dinner cruises on double-decker

BEALE STREET LANDING

What: Riverboat dock and recreational space

Where: 251 Riverside Dr.

Cost: Free to visit; day/dinner cruises vary

Pro tip: Look for festivals and events hosted at Beale Street Landing on a regular basis.

One way to quickly tell the river's water level is to take a look at the circular red loading ramp at Beale Street Landing. When the water's low, you can see all the ramp's twists; at times, only the top part of the ramp is visible.

A sunny day at Beale Street Landing brings out joggers, cyclists, and families. Inset: *The* Island Queen *riverboat is used for sightseeing tours, dinner cruises, and private charters.*

paddlewheelers that leave and return in a few hours, while the American Queen Steamboat Company offers the kind of Mark Twain-ish steamboat adventure that lasts days or weeks, with stops in Memphis.

If you're not embarking on a river cruise, Beale Street Landing is still worth a visit. Kids love playing on the hill (a sign warns that the slope "exceeds 8 percent," which stops exactly no one from trying to roll or slide down it), and there are paths for walking and biking. When the weather's warm, there's a small splash park with a giant catfish named "Big John."

REMEMBER NATCH THE BEAR

What was the first animal at the Memphis Zoo?

As one of the top-rated zoos in the country, the Memphis Zoo doesn't qualify as a secret. But this nationally acclaimed attraction has some odd history, long before its days of state-of-the-art animal habitats and educational programs.

Back in 1905, it was acceptable—at least in one instance—for a bear to serve as payment between businessmen, and that's how Colonel Robert Galloway found himself caring for a Southern black bear named Natch. While the bear's living conditions were disturbing by today's standards, the truth is that Natch started his Memphis tenure tied to a tree in Overton Park, surrounded by a small fence. Acknowledging the unsuitable lodging

MEMPHIS ZOO'S NATCH THE BEAR

What: Monument at the Memphis Zoo

Where: 2000 Prentiss Pl.

Cost: Adults ages 12-59, $18; children ages 2-11, $13; seniors 60+, $17; parking, $5

Pro tip: Natch is the inspiration for the Memphis Grizzlies' alternate mascot, who plays the villain opposite the official mascot, Grizz. You can watch the two bears wrestle each other in WWE-style ring matches during wrestling theme nights at Grizzlies NBA games.

Natch was the mascot for a baseball team called the Memphis Turtles, and the first fundraiser for the Memphis Zoological Society was a baseball game.

NEAR THIS SPOT IN 1905
"NATCH" THE BLACK BEAR
CREATED PUBLIC INTEREST
RESULTING IN THE FOUNDING OF
MEMPHIS ZOOLOGICAL GARDEN
APRIL 4, 1906
ERECTED ON THIS 75TH ANNIVERSARY BY
MEMPHIS ZOOLOGICAL SOCIETY
APRIL 4, 1981

The Natch monument was installed in 1981. Photo courtesy Joseph Miner via the Memphis Zoo.

arrangements for little Natch, Galloway began to raise funds for what would eventually become the Memphis Zoological Society. The society first built bear dens and enclosures for Natch and other rescued wild animals, then constructed buildings for big cats and elephants.

These days the Memphis Zoo focuses on conservation, education, and research and is home to hundreds of animals, including at least four kinds of bears. See grizzly bears in the four-acre Teton Trek exhibit, watch polar bears swim and black bears frolic in the Northwest Passage, and visit the zoo's two pandas, Ya Ya and Le Le, in the China exhibit.

A monument near the entrance of Primate Canyon marks the spot where Natch once resided and "created public interest" that founded the Memphis Zoological Society. It was built on the seventy-fifth anniversary of the zoo.

LADY LIBERTY, MEMPHIS EDITION

Why is there a replica of the Statue of Liberty on Winchester?

If you ever drive past what appears to be the Statue of Liberty in Memphis, you haven't gone crazy and your eyes aren't playing tricks on you. There really is a seventy-two-foot version of the national monument at the intersection of Winchester and Kirby, albeit with some changes in accessories.

The statue, erected on July 4, 2006, by the World Overcomers Outreach Ministries Church, features the six-story-tall Lady Liberty we know, except instead of a torch symbolizing enlightenment, she wields an enormous Christian cross. Instead of a tablet, she holds the Ten Commandments. The statue's gold crown reads "Jehovah," and she has a tear rolling down her cheek. Her official name, according to the church, is *Statue of Liberation Through Christ*. Unlike the statue in New York City, which is more than three hundred feet tall and cast in copper, the Memphis version is made of fiberglass.

The World Overcomers Church's leader, Apostle Alton R. Williams, writes on the church's website that the $260,000

The *New York Times* covered the statue's unveiling in a July 5, 2006, article and reported that it cost $260,000 to build and install.

STATUE OF LIBERATION THROUGH CHRIST

What: A Christianized version of the Statue of Liberty

Where: 6655 Winchester Rd.

Cost: Free to see

Pro tip: Take care if you try to take photos; the statue is in front of the megachurch and just a few feet away from a major intersection.

monument was built to "cause people to remember [the United States'] Christian heritage." It's a spectacle that causes many drivers to look twice, but longtime Memphians just know it as "that weird Statue of Liberty on Winchester."

155

THE WITHERS COLLECTION

Why does one of America's greatest photographers have a gallery on Beale?

You can see a lot of things walking down Beale Street, from street buskers to enormous beers to young men doing backflips over huddled volunteers. But what you might not expect is a photography gallery featuring images that changed the world.

Photographer Dr. Ernest Withers started his career as an Army photographer and Memphis police officer, pursuing freelance photojournalism on the side. He's best known for his images of civil rights era people and events, but he also captured the world's beloved musicians (Elvis Presley, B. B. King), black athletes such as Jackie Robinson, and everyday life in Memphis.

He became involved in the civil rights movement when he published photos of the murder of fourteen-year-old African American Emmett Till in Mississippi in 1955. Withers went on to photograph the Montgomery Bus Boycott, the Memphis Sanitation Workers' Strike, and many other

---

Today the gallery on Beale is open most afternoons and showcases a rotating selection of work from different eras of Withers's work.

The Withers Collection Museum and Gallery is located next to the Old Daisy theater and across the street from the New Daisy theater.

important moments. Throughout his sixty-year career, Withers created more than 1.8 million images, some of which are on display at a gallery and museum at the site of his longtime studio on Beale Street.

WITHERS COLLECTION MUSEUM & GALLERY

What: The work of a prolific Memphis photojournalist

Where: 333 Beale St.

Cost: Adults, $10; students and seniors, $7

Pro tip: Check ahead for gallery hours, which may change due to holidays or events.

DOWNTOWN'S ANTIQUE MYSTERIES

What can I find in Victorian Village?

In downtown Memphis, amid the neighborhoods, shops, and healthcare facilities of the Medical District, there's a row of ornate Victorian homes called Victorian Village. It's what's left of Millionaire's Row, the hottest Memphis suburb of the late 1800s. There are a handful of historic homes in various stages of preservation on the street, including three museums, one upscale bed-and-breakfast, and a nightclub.

VICTORIAN VILLAGE

What: Historic district featuring Victorian homes

Where: Adams Avenue, between Danny Thomas Boulevard and Manassas Street

Cost: Varies

Pro tip: For luxurious lodgings, reserve a room at the lavish James Lee House bed and breakfast.

Every corner in Victorian Village has its own backstory or secret to tell. For example, while the Woodruff-Fontaine House stands out as a stunning example of a restored and historically furnished Victorian home, it's also said to be haunted by multiple ghosts including Mollie Woodruff, who lived in the home in the late 1800s. The Mallory-Neely House may have less

The Magevney House is another museum in Victorian Village. The 1830s cottage is free to visitors and is open the first Saturday of the month.

The Mallory-Neely House was built in the Italianate villa style, and almost all of the features are original. Inset: The Woodruff-Fontaine House and adjacent James Lee House are listed together on the National Register of Historic Places.

paranormal activity, but it housed residents as recently as 1969 when Daisy Neely Mallory passed away at age ninety-eight. She kept much of the Victorian decor and furnishing intact, including the elegant stained-glass windows purchased at the 1893 Chicago World's Fair.

You can encounter another kind of spirit at Mollie Fontaine Lounge, a Victorian home converted into a bar and nightclub. Open in the evenings only, Mollie's offers cocktails and dinner, dancing, and shows.

SOUL FOOD IN SOULSVILLE

What's the history behind the Four Way restaurant?

The Four Way is not only a soul food restaurant, it's a Memphis institution and the hub of the Soulsville neighborhood in South Memphis. For almost seventy-five years, locals, tourists, celebrities, and dignitaries have dined at its tables, enjoying delicacies such as fried catfish, fried chicken, and turkey and dressing, plus Southern veggies such as greens, okra, and yams.

Back before the daily specials and meat-and-threes, the building was a pool hall and shoe repair shop. In 1946 Irene and Clint Cleaves purchased the place and began serving home-cooked meals, later adding a dining room in the back. To sit in the dining room customers had to ring the doorbell and be admitted by staff, but this was more for show than for exclusivity. In fact, the Four Way was one of

THE FOUR WAY

What: Historic restaurant in South Memphis

Where: 998 Mississippi Blvd.

Cost: Depends

Pro tip: The Four Way's proximity to the Stax Museum makes it the perfect post-tour meal.

The list of celebrities who dined at the Four Way includes Reverend Al Green, Gladys Knight, Ike and Tina Turner, and more recently Drake.

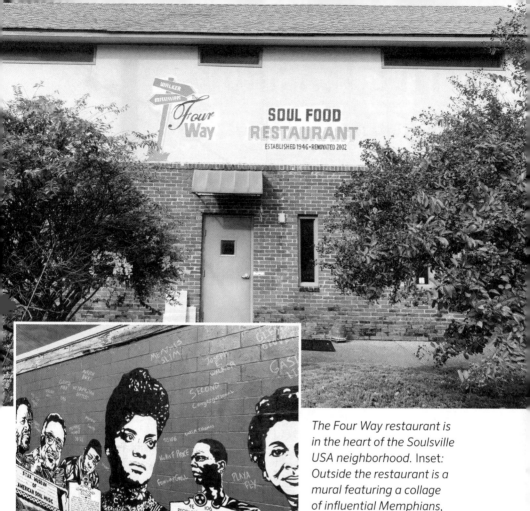

SOUL FOOD
RESTAURANT
ESTABLISHED 1946 • RENOVATED 2002

The Four Way restaurant is in the heart of the Soulsville USA neighborhood. Inset: Outside the restaurant is a mural featuring a collage of influential Memphians, including Ida B. Wells.

the only places in town where black and white citizens could eat together, attracting everyone from musicians such as Elvis Presley and Aretha Franklin to civil rights leaders such as Dr. Martin Luther King Jr. and Reverend Jesse Jackson.

The Four Way remained a constant source of community and comfort food for decades, but it closed in 1996. Six years later, Soulsville native Willie Earl Bates bought the Four Way at auction, renovated the space, and reopened with Irene Cleaves's recipes. His daughter Patrice Bates Thompson continues the tradition today, minus the secret doorbell.

LITTLE TEA SHOP

Does the Little Tea Shop serve tea?

Every weekday in Memphis, downtown professionals flock to a humble eatery on Monroe Avenue. The restaurant is filled to the brim with longtime regulars, many of whom have claimed their table for years. Don't worry, though—owner Suhair Lauck makes sure there's plenty of room for new visitors to pull up a chair and try the classic Southern dishes.

The original Little Tea Shop was founded by Emily A. Carpenter and Lillie E. Parham in 1918, and was purchased by Vernon Mortimer Bell after World War II. Mr. Bell sold the business to Ms. Lauck in the 1980s. His family is still in the restaurant business: they own the popular Mortimer's restaurant in East Memphis.

More cozy café than hole-in-the-wall, the Little Tea Shop still feels like a secret even after one hundred years in business. The current owner—called "Miss Sue" by regular customers—has run the place like a well-oiled machine since

LITTLE TEA SHOP

What: One-hundred-year-old restaurant in downtown Memphis

Where: 69 Monroe Ave.

Cost: Depends

Pro tip: The restaurant is open for lunch only on weekdays.

Corn sticks are a form of cornbread cooked in a cast iron pan with narrow molds, which keeps the outside of the bread crispy and the inside soft and piping hot. They are the Little Tea Shop's signature item.

In the mid-twentieth century, workers from the nearby Memphis Cotton Exchange established The Little Tea Shop as a convenient lunch spot.

the '80s, greeting diners at the door and running the cash register with warmth and energy.

As for the food, the Little Tea Shop's menu changes daily with specials such as Hoppin' John (black-eyed peas and rice) or Moroccan chicken (baked with herbs and spices). Some menu items are served every day, such as the Lacy's Special, a chicken breast sandwiched between corn sticks and smothered with gravy.

MASON TEMPLE

Where did Dr. King give his "I've Been to the Mountaintop" speech?

A tour of Memphis civil rights locations always rightfully includes the National Civil Rights Museum at the Lorraine Motel. The museum is built at the site of Dr. Martin Luther King Jr.'s assassination and includes powerful, interactive exhibits that tell the story of civil rights not just from a Memphis perspective, but encompassing the worldwide struggle for equality.

What is not always on the tour is the Mason Temple, the church that played an integral part in the civil rights movement in the United States.

The Mason Temple has served as the world headquarters for the Church of God in Christ since its dedication in 1945. The building, designed by church member William Harrison Taylor, took five years to

MASON TEMPLE

What: Site of Dr. King's last speech

Where: 930 Mason St.

Cost: Free

Pro tip: A Tour of Possibilities offers unique, personal van tours of civil rights sites and Memphis history, including the Mason Temple.

The building is a part of the National Register of Historic Places, the US Civil Rights Trail, and the Memphis Heritage Trail.

The public is allowed to tour on weekdays from 9 a.m. to 4 p.m. unless the church is hosting a special event, but it's always a good idea to call ahead to confirm.

complete due to supply rations in World War II. The temple is named after COGIC's Bishop Charles H. Mason, who founded the Church of God in Christ in 1897; today the church has more than six million members across the world.

In the 1960s, civil rights leaders used the church as a meeting place for the Sanitation Workers Strike. Dr. King delivered his famous "Mountaintop" speech to the congregation at the Mason Temple on the evening of April 3, 1968, the night before he was assassinated at the Lorraine Motel.

MEMPHIS SLIM HOUSE

Who was Memphis Slim and where is his house?

Before young musicians flocked to the Slim House in Soulsville to collaborate and record, the site was home to blues legend Memphis Slim. Born John Chatman in 1915, Slim grew up in a family of blues musicians from the Mississippi Delta. He taught himself to play piano and started singing in juke joints and dance halls on Beale Street and across the region while living in the two-story house in South Memphis.

In 1939 he moved to Chicago and worked as a dependable session pianist and dynamic live performer. Eventually he took up the nickname "Memphis Slim" after his hometown. After World War II Slim started his own band, the House Rockers, and released "Every Day I Have The Blues," a blues standard later covered by the likes of B.

> ### MEMPHIS SLIM HOUSE
>
> **What:** Music incubator and community center
>
> **Where:** 1130 College St.
>
> **Cost:** Free to see
>
> **Pro tip:** The Stax Museum is across the street from the Slim House, so be sure to see both when you're in the area.

The original home did not survive because of its poor condition and safety concerns. The new building—designed by Memphis architect Jason Jackson—sits on the same space and uses salvaged bricks from the original fireplace.

The Memphis Slim House uses an affordable membership model to provide support and resources for the community.

B. King, Ray Charles, and Ella Fitzgerald. He lived most of his life in Paris, France, and recorded more than five hundred blues songs.

Meanwhile, his former home sat deteriorating for decades. In 2014 local organizations including the nearby LeMoyne-Owen College, the University of Memphis, and Community LIFT came together to save the property. The rebuilt home opened as a community space where up-and-coming artists can meet, collaborate, record music, and host events.

CORNELIA'S WORDS

Where is the *She Spoke Her Mind* mural?

Memphis is full of bright and bold murals, and every time you think you've found them all, another one appears. The neon letters proclaiming "She Spoke Her Mind" on a library wall are still flying under the radar when it comes to social media, but the mural is so much more than just a colorful Instagram post. It stands for the words of the unsung hero of civil rights in Memphis, the late Cornelia Crenshaw.

As smaller community libraries dwindle in numbers, this branch remains a stalwart in the community. Originally called the Cossitt Library for Negroes, this library was established in 1939 as the first library for black Memphians during segregation. Renamed the Vance Avenue Library in 1960, the building burned down in 1978 but was rebuilt. It was renamed in 1997 to honor the work of the activist, a graduate of Booker T. Washington High School and Lemoyne-Owen College.

Crenshaw supported the Sanitation Workers' Strike of 1968, distributing food to the strikers and providing support. Crenshaw was one of the many women who helped lead the civil rights movement of the 1960s, especially the Sanitation Workers' Strike.

The library is a part of the Memphis Women's Legacy Trail and the Historic Commerce Loop of the Memphis Heritage Trail.

168

Ms. Crenshaw advocated for community equity and fair payment for utilities in Memphis. She lived in the neighborhood and frequented this library before her death in 1994.

CORNELIA CRENSHAW MEMORIAL LIBRARY

What: Mural inspired by a civil rights leader

Where: 531 Vance Ave.

Cost: Free to visit

Pro tip: Find more civil rights-inspired murals on South Main Street and in other spots around downtown Memphis.

It was she who, inspired by the words from her friend Robert Worsham's poem, suggested the pointed yet simple slogan for that strike: "I AM A MAN."

SOUL WOMEN

Who were the women of Stax Records?

Even if you didn't know it came from Memphis, you're certainly familiar with the Stax sound: the whistling melody of Otis Redding's "(Sittin' On) The Dock of the Bay," the smooth grooves from Isaac Hayes's "Theme from Shaft" and *Hot Buttered Soul*, and Sam and Dave's soulful duos such as "Hold On, I'm Comin'" and "Soul Man." These soul artists made a well-earned name for themselves and for Stax. But there are always a few stories that get lost in the shuffle; in this case, there are the women of Stax.

In fact, the name "Stax" comes from the combined first letters of brother-and-sister label cofounders Jim Stewart and Estelle Axton. Estelle had an ear for popular music, spending time at record shops

Another star from Stax is Mavis Staples, whose seven-decade career includes hits with the Staple Singers, award-winning solo albums, high-profile collaborations, and a touring schedule that continues today.

The Stax Museum is a replica of the original Capital Theater that housed the recording studio and record shop from the late 1950s to 1976.

and discovering new artists. She took out a second mortgage on her home to help fund the fledgling recording service and became an integral part of the Stax label.

Estelle also opened the Satellite Record Store adjacent to the recording studio in South Memphis and later founded the Memphis Songwriters Association. Shirley Brown was the last artist to earn a number-one song for Stax with her 1974 smash hit "Woman to Woman," which sold a million copies and got her a Grammy nomination. Other women, such as soul singer Carla Thomas and musician-turned-music-PR-pro Deanie Parker, were integral parts of the Stax story.

ONE-STOP CULTURAL SHOP

What is the Center for Southern Folklore?

Part museum, part gift shop, and part café, the Center for Southern Folklore on Main Street fills a niche for Memphis music, art, and history. Since 1972 the center and its cofounder Judy Peiser have collected films, recordings, photos, articles, and artifacts that document the life of people in Memphis and the Delta. Started as a private nonprofit arts organization, the center occupied several spaces on Beale Street in the 1990s before moving to Main Street in 1999.

While you're there, you can peruse the archives and discover even more Memphis secrets and stories from the documents collected within. You can also have a beer, hear some good music, and do a little shopping to support the arts. The Center for Southern Folklore hosts live music nights, usually on Saturdays, and has a small stage in a room with about forty seats at tables.

The center serves up Southern comfort food if you get hungry while you're there—the mac 'n' cheese, greens, and peach cobbler are longtime favorites. Need to find some one-of-a-kind souvenirs, local art, or CDs? The Center for Southern Folklore has an inventory of just that. It's a one-stop shop hidden in plain sight on Main Street.

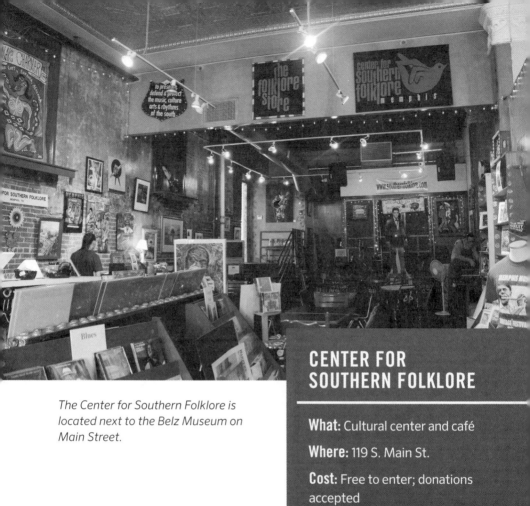

The Center for Southern Folklore is located next to the Belz Museum on Main Street.

CENTER FOR SOUTHERN FOLKLORE

What: Cultural center and café

Where: 119 S. Main St.

Cost: Free to enter; donations accepted

Pro tip: Look up the center's live music schedule at southernfolklore.com.

Heritage Hall is another area within the center for film screenings and dance and music performances.

THE ANTENNA

Did Memphis ever have a punk rock scene?

You know that Memphis is a hotbed for all things rock 'n' roll, soul, and blues. But Memphis has always had a bit of a punk streak too. The Sex Pistols played in Memphis in 1978 (see secret #42), and the city's alternative music scene was never the same.

The Antenna might have been the place that inspired the term "hole-in-the-wall" because, by all accounts, that's all it was. The dark, seedy spot that was Memphis's first real punk club came alive in 1981, when owner Steve McGehee took over, and closed its doors in 1995. In between, many punk legends graced its stage.

The club was a home for original music, for teens seeking the punk scene, and for newfangled music videos on TVs set up around the bar. The roster of bands who played there is impressive. Acts such as R.E.M., Black Flag, Red Hot Chili Peppers, Green Day, Flaming Lips, and the Replacements, plus plenty of local Memphis bands including the Grifters, the Oblivians, Impala, and all-girl punk group the Klitz, performed or got their start at the Antenna.

**THE ANTENNA — AN ORIGINAL
PUNK ROCK VENUE**

The Antenna, otherwise known as "Memphis's original
punk rock club," operated on this site at 1588 Madison
from 1981 to 1995. Before The Antenna, nightspots
under other names — "The Library," "The Mousetrap,"
"Detroit Rock City," and "The Well" — were in business
at this address. After the Sex Pistols performed in
Memphis on January 6, 1978, "The Well" featured local
bands as early as 1979 and it was the starting point for
an underground music scene that The Antenna adopted
and expanded. The Antenna opened on June 26, 1981,
under the ownership of Steve McGehee, who would
break new ground to elevate and energize the music
scene in Memphis and place it on the national map and
beyond. McGehee based the name of the club on
television sets that had "rabbit ear" antennas. David
Fisher designed the club's logo.

SPONSORED BY CINDY AND STEVE MCGEHEE, ADRIENNE AND JOHN LITTLEFIELD,
AND THE SHELBY COUNTY HISTORICAL COMMISSION • OCTOBER, 2019

In late 2019 the city placed a marker on the
site of the former club, detailing a short
history of the bar's music legacy.

A HAUNTED BROTHEL ON MAIN STREET

What happened at Earnestine & Hazel's?

It's the 1960s in Memphis, and after a concert at downtown's Club Paradise, you head to the after-hours club: Earnestine & Hazel's. Named for the co-owners (who were given the building by Coppertone mogul Abe Plough), it was a seedy jazz club with a beauty salon and a brothel upstairs. For years, artists like Aretha Franklin and Ray Charles would hang out after shows at the E&H for drinks and fun.

Fast forward to 1993, when Russell George takes over the failing brothel and turns it into a legitimate operation. He serves just one menu item: a simple griddle cheeseburger he calls the Soul Burger. He ignores the ghost sightings and the jukebox that plays random songs without warning.

For decades, Russell and his staff—including bartenders Karen Brownlee and Nathaniel Barnes—make Earnestine & Hazel's the epitome of a beloved

EARNESTINE & HAZEL'S

What: Historic, haunted dive bar

Where: 531 S. Main St.

Cost: Varies

Pro tip: For the morning after, head to the Arcade Restaurant across the street for a vintage-style diner frequented by Elvis; it serves the best sweet potato pancakes and milkshakes, and it has a full bar too.

Don't skip the Soul Burger, served with your choice of a single or double patty and a bag of Golden Flake Thin & Crispy chips.

E&H is at the historic corner of South Main Street and G. E. Patterson Avenue, opposite the Central Station hotel and train station.

dive bar. It's welcoming to regulars playing pool, visitors seeking ghost stories, and late-night revelers who stumble through the small upstairs rooms to find Mr. Nate serving liquor drinks at his bar. Even through Russell's passing in 2012, new owners, staff changes, and structural repairs to the building, the spirit, environment, and menu remain mostly unchanged.

Earnestine & Hazel's is on every "haunted places" and "dive bar" listicle to come out in the last decade, it's been in the movies, and its paranormal qualities are documented by every wannabe ghostbuster east and west of the Mississippi. And yet, when you step inside, you still feel like you're discovering a local secret.

The place is like a sponge, able to absorb all the fame and notoriety without losing its signature clandestine vibe. It might be easier to ask, "What *hasn't* happened at Earnestine & Hazel's?"

EGYPTIAN CONNECTION

What does Memphis, Tennessee, have in common with ancient Egypt?

Memphis is named after an African city on the banks of the Nile River: Memphis, Egypt, nestled in the Nile Delta, was the ancient capital of Lower Egypt. The Tennessee city, named in 1819 by explorers who saw the geographical connections to the Egyptian Memphis, gives a nod to its namesake in several ways.

The most famous is, of course, the giant glass pyramid that's now home to a Bass Pro Shops. When the Memphis Pyramid opened in 1991, the Egyptian government gave the city permission to build a twenty-five-foot-tall fiberglass replica of the famous Ramesses the Great statue, which was discovered in the ruins of the ancient city in the 1800s.

For decades, Ramesses stood guard over the Pyramid, which hosted basketball games, concerts, and wrestling events until the building became vacant in 2004. As preparations were made for the Pyramid's reopening as outdoor megaretailer Bass Pro, it became clear that the Egyptian king needed a more appropriate home.

Anyone driving down Central Avenue by the University of Memphis may see the statue, but most don't make the connection between the city, the university's Egyptian Art and Archaeology program, the replica's history, and the mummies on display on campus.

Entrance to the Art Museum of the University of Memphis.

RAMESSES THE GREAT STATUE

What: Statue of Ramesses the Great

Where: University of Memphis, Central Avenue

Cost: Free to see

Pro tip: When the museum is not closed for exhibition changes or maintenance, it's open Monday through Saturday from 9 a.m. to 5 p.m. and is free and open to the public.

In 2012 the Memphis City Council voted to move him a few miles away to the University of Memphis, where he stands today. Since 1987 the university has operated the renowned Institute of Egyptian Art and Archaeology. The institute also manages the Egyptian Gallery at the Art Museum of the University of Memphis, where more than fourteen hundred Egyptian artifacts—including real mummies—are on display.

THE PINCH DISTRICT

Why is it called the "Pinch District"?

There's one Memphis neighborhood that is home to a world-renowned hospital, a giant glass pyramid, beloved restaurants, and historic buildings looking for new life: the Pinch District. Only two miles from the tourists, musicians, and revelry on Beale Street, you'll discover this intriguing area. The district's first residents were a melting pot of Irish immigrants, settlers from Central and Eastern Europe, and a Jewish community that thrived there in pre-World War II Memphis.

What makes the area unique is a mix of history, architecture, beloved institutions, and the capacity for imminent growth and change. With a colossal, modern glass pyramid, a world-class research hospital on the verge of a $1 billion expansion, and historic buildings—some occupied by restaurants and businesses and others that still need to be saved—the neighborhood has a variety of cultures and plenty of potential.

There are a few stops on your Pinch tour that are beloved by locals but still feel like hidden gems. Alcenia's has fed hungry Memphians and visitors with a side of Southern hospitality since 1997. Owner B. J. Chester-Tamayo greets guests with a hug before she whips up a homestyle meal of fried catfish, meatloaf, greens, cornbread, cobbler, and other

The name comes from an insensitive nickname for the Irish inhabitants, who reportedly had a "pinched gut" appearance due to hunger and malnutrition caused by the Irish potato famine.

Alcenia's sits in the shadow of the Bass Pro Pyramid.

THE PINCH DISTRICT

What: Eclectic, historic, up-and-coming neighborhood

Where: North downtown Memphis, east of the Wolf River Harbor

Cost: Free to explore

Pro tip: A few relative newcomers to the Pinch include the Office at Uptown and Comeback Coffee, both cozy coffee shops perfect for a cup of joe.

soul food favorites that have earned her restaurant a spot on the *New York Times*'s two hundred places to visit in the United States.

Swing by Westy's for lunch or a late-night meal and a drink or two. The Memphis institution, helmed since 1983 by Jake Schorr, boasts an enormous menu, including the famous Hot Fudge Pie, and offers late-night eats and delivery.

MODEL OF THE MIGHTY MISSISSIPPI

What are Mud Island River Park's secrets?

The first thing to know about Mud Island is that it's not actually an island. Mud Island is a peninsula, home to the Harbor Town community on the northern part of the peninsula and Mud Island River Park to the south.

If you visit this downtown Memphis "island" you can walk along the banks of a tiny version of the Lower Mississippi River, from Cairo, Illinois, to the Gulf of Mexico. The topographically accurate map of the second-longest river in North America is scaled down to about the length of five city blocks and shows cities, towns, and bridges along the river's path, as well

MUD ISLAND RIVER PARK

What: Mini-Mississippi River model, *The Firm* filming location, and an Insta hot spot

Where: 125 North Front St.

Cost: Free to visit Mud Island; Mississippi River Museum is open May to October; admission for adults 12 and over, $10; children ages 4–11, $8; children under 4, free

Pro tip: Access Mud Island via the Skybridge (walk, bike, or scooter) or drive in through the Northern Gate.

Mud Island is home to a five-thousand-seat amphitheater in addition to the seasonal Mississippi River Museum. The Memphis River Parks Partnership hosts free music and community events there.

At Mud Island River Park, catch views of downtown Memphis's skyline and the Hernando de Soto Bridge.

as a scale model of the city of Memphis. The river model ends south of New Orleans, with the "Gulf of Mexico" represented by a large pool that's used for paddleboarding during the warmer months.

The mini-Mississippi isn't Mud Island's only claim to fame. In the 1993 film *The Firm*, Tom Cruise's character rides the Skybridge monorail that connects downtown Memphis to Mud Island. If you've seen people pose for social media photos in front of a giant white "MEMPHIS" sign by the river and wondered where to find the sculpture, it's located at Mud Island River Park. The sign was installed in honor of Memphis's bicentennial in 2019.

HOT RODS IN THE EDGE

What happened down the street from Sun Studio?

Besides Graceland and the National Civil Rights Museum, Sun Studio is probably the most famous site for music history in Memphis. A pilgrimage to the small recording studio in the Edge District is a must for any Memphis or Elvis lover. Sun Studio is where Elvis recorded his first song, where Sam Phillips developed the sound forever known as rock 'n' roll, and where the Million Dollar Quartet—Elvis, Johnny Cash, Carl Perkins, and Jerry Lee Lewis—posed for the now-famous photo of their brief jam session.

But what else was happening while Elvis and other music legends cut their teeth (and cut albums) at Sun? The neighborhood's strange angular street layout is evidence of its start as a railroad hub, and the industrial area later attracted automotive repair shops, hot rod garages, and artist workspaces. Today it's a mix of established businesses, historic sites, and newer attractions such as High Cotton Brewing Company and the Edge Motor Museum.

Opened in 2019, the Edge Motor Museum is in the former Saint Blues Guitar Workshop just steps away from Sun Studio. Inside, you can learn about the thirty-year heyday of American sports cars that began after World War II. The small but thorough museum provides the historical and cultural context

---

Can't get enough hot rods? Complete your exploration into Memphis rock and car culture at the Elvis Presley Automobile Museum at Graceland.

The Edge Motor Museum is just around the corner from Sun Studio.

EDGE MOTOR MUSEUM

What: Museum showcasing the history of the American sports car

Where: 645 Marshall Ave.

Cost: Adults, $10; children, $5

Pro tip: While you're in the neighborhood, grab a bite to eat at Edge Alley, Chef Tam's Underground Café, or Evelyn & Olive, or stop into one of the other shops and galleries.

of the sports car—think the refined lines of an early Ford Thunderbird; the original Ford Mustang, America's ultimate pony car; or the odd styling of the Avanti, a Studebaker spin-off.

Best of all, the museum has hot rods and classic art on display that are sure to delight gearheads and rockabilly culture lovers. The car lineup changes regularly, and you can truly get to know each vehicle through informational iPads or from helpful museum docents. Word is still getting out about the Edge Motor Museum, a small but mighty stop on a Memphis culture and history tour in the Edge District.

OVERTON PARK OLD FOREST

Where is the only urban old-growth forest in the Southeastern United States?

Two facts make the incredible Overton Park Old Forest unique. The first is that the forest is the only urban old-growth forest in the Southeast. The second is that it represents a ten-thousand-year-old ecosystem, and some of the trees are more than two hundred years old. This historic place is nestled in the middle of a bustling city, surrounded by roads, neighborhoods, and businesses.

The other bit of history that makes the Old Forest special to Memphis is this: it exists only because a group of concerned citizens fought for its preservation. In the fifties and sixties, the Federal Highway Administration attempted to build Interstate 40 directly through Overton Park, destroying forest lands and bisecting the city. Citizens to Preserve Overton Park formed to fight the construction of the road, and after losing initial court cases, appealed for an emergency Supreme Court ruling that would save the park.

The 142-acre forest is a State Natural Area, is on the National Register of Historic Places, and is a certified arboretum with more than thirty species of trees, three hundred species of plants, and plenty of wildlife.

The Old Forest has paved and unpaved trails for biking, running, and walking.

The group's victory became a landmark case studied in law programs around the country, and it marked one of the first times a nonprofit would defeat a US federal agency in court. Thanks to the efforts of engaged Memphians, I-40 takes a detour around the central part of the city, and Overton Park exists as a communal space with paved and unpaved trails, gardens, a playground, a lake, a public golf course, dog parks, the Memphis Zoo, Veterans Plaza, and historic buildings such as the Memphis College of Art and the Memphis Brooks Museum of Art. The Overton Park Conservancy manages, maintains, and protects the park.

MACHINE GUN KELLY'S LAST HIDEOUT

Was Machine Gun Kelly arrested in Memphis?

George Kelly Barnes was born in 1895 in Memphis, Tennessee. He attended Central High School and went on to live a very interesting life. On a September morning in 1933, FBI agents raided a house on Rayner Street in Memphis, arresting George and his wife, Kathryn, on charges of kidnapping.

You probably know George better as Machine Gun Kelly, the notorious Prohibition-era gangster who kidnapped, bootlegged, and robbed his way through the United States brandishing a Thompson machine gun. He began his career bootlegging illegal booze in Memphis, then spent time in Oklahoma and Kansas before he endeavored to kidnap the wealthy Charles L. Urschel for ransom.

It was this kidnapping that led Kelly and his wife to hide out in a nondescript home in Memphis, and what led agents to capture and convict both of them. Kelly spent his life in prison at Alcatraz and in the federal penitentiary in Leavenworth, Kansas. His wife was released from prison in 1958 and lived until 1985.

Machine Gun Kelly was said to hang out in a downtown speakeasy that became the Green Beetle bar not long after he was arrested.

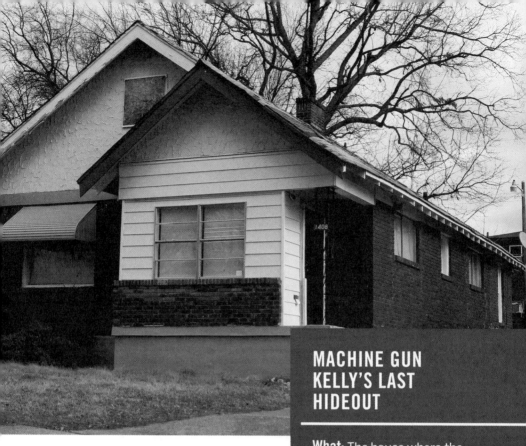

The home where Machine Gun Kelly and his wife were arrested in 1933.

While there's not much to see and nothing to set apart the home on Rayner Street, it's still a Memphis secret that this is where the illustrious career of a notorious gangster came to a relatively quiet end.

MACHINE GUN KELLY'S LAST HIDEOUT

What: The house where the notorious gangster was finally arrested

Where: 1408 Rayner St.

Cost: Free to see

Pro tip: The home is in a quiet neighborhood, so be quick and respectful on your visit.

TRAGEDY AT THE LORRAINE

Where was Martin Luther King Jr. assassinated?

Most people know that civil rights leader Dr. Martin Luther King Jr. was assassinated in Memphis, but not everyone is familiar with the circumstances that brought him to the city, nor the way that his life and work are commemorated on the site of the National Civil Rights Museum at the Lorraine Motel.

King visited Memphis in April 1968 to support the Memphis Sanitation Workers' Strike, which protested the deadly working conditions and unfair labor practices faced by black Memphis workers. He gave his famous "I've Been to the Mountaintop" speech at the Mason Temple in Memphis on the evening of April 3. On the morning of the next day, King was standing on the balcony of

NATIONAL CIVIL RIGHTS MUSEUM

What: Site of Dr. Martin Luther King Jr.'s assassination

Where: 450 Mulberry St.

Cost: Adults, $17; students and seniors with ID, $15; children 5-17, $14; children 4 and under, free; active US military, free

Pro tip: The museum is open daily from 9 a.m. to 5 p.m., except Tuesdays.

The Legacy Building adjacent to the museum contains two exhibits: one focused on the assassination's investigation, aftermath, and conspiracy theories and the other on global civil rights efforts that continue today.

The plaza at the Lorraine Motel and commemorative wreath. Left: The eye-catching sign is a replica of the original motel's futuristic Googie-style design, which was influenced by car culture and the Space Age and was popular in the fifties and sixties.

the Lorraine Motel when he was shot and killed. James Earl Ray was convicted of his murder in 1969.

The site of King's assassination is marked by a white and red wreath on the balcony of the motel, part of which is preserved to look as it did when King stayed there. In fact, the room where he stayed is preserved exactly as it was when he stepped out of it that morning. Anyone can visit the plaza and observe the wreath.

The museum opened in 1991, closed in 2012 for renovations, and reopened in 2014 with interactive exhibits, artifacts, and moving immersive displays. The museum not only tells the story of King's involvement in the Memphis civil rights movement but also provides context for the movement within the story of civil rights. It begins with the American slave trade and continues through the civil rights era, featuring the individuals and groups who fought for justice.

THE INFLUENCE OF ARDENT

Who wrote the theme song for *That '70s Show*?

Music fans around the world know and love Memphis for its impact on rock 'n' roll and soul music, but the influence of music and musicians extends far beyond Elvis.

Ardent Studios is the perfect example of this. Started by radio-loving Memphis teenagers, including founder John Fry, Ardent began as a garage recording studio in 1966. In the early-to-mid-seventies, R&B label Stax Records partnered with the team at Ardent to record overflow sessions with the Staple Singers, Isaac Hayes, Sam and Dave, and many more.

Mentored by the passionate Ardent owner, musicians Alex Chilton, Chris Bell, Jody Stephens, and Andy Hummel recorded their debut album, *#1 Record*, as a band called Big Star in 1972. The record received rave reviews, and, along with Big Star's subsequent two albums, is attributed with pioneering the "power pop" sound, but the release flopped due to distribution issues.

Big Star experienced some revived attention with reissues of their records in the late seventies and a CD release in the nineties. One single from *#1 Record*, called "In the Street," fit the exact mood for the Fox sitcom *That '70s Show*, which

---

In the late eighties Ardent launched a Christian rock label and produced some of the most successful Christian albums of the 1990s with bands such as Big Tent Revival and Skillet.

Ardent Studios is just west of Overton Square entertainment district.

ARDENT RECORDING STUDIO

What: Influential music recording studio in Midtown

Where: 2000 Madison Ave.

Cost: Free to see

Pro tip: Contact the studio directly for tours.

used versions of the song sung by the show's cast and later by rock band Cheap Trick, as its theme song. The original version was of course recorded right in the heart of Memphis at Ardent Studios.

Bands looking for a specific sound continued to come to Memphis to record at Ardent, including Led Zeppelin, ZZ Top, R.E.M., James Taylor, B. B. King, the Replacements, and later Three 6 Mafia, the White Stripes, Cat Power, and more.

In its own quiet way, the studio started by three friends who loved music continued to influence the biggest names in rock and pop while remaining largely unknown to the casual music fan.

A MEMPHIS ART TOUR

What's the story behind Memphis's many murals?

Memphis has thousands of murals across nearly every neighborhood. Some are enormous public art projects, while others are hidden emblems and street art on forgotten corners. This is a sampling of a few of them.

Around the corner from the National Civil Rights Museum, the 2016 mural *Memphis Upstanders* features images of influential Memphians who stood up for their fellow citizens and spoke out against injustice. The organization Facing History and Ourselves facilitated the selection of the fourteen individuals portrayed on the wall, including antilynching activist and journalist Ida B. Wells, victim of the 1866 Memphis Massacre Lucy Tibbs, and Jewish leader and civil rights activist Rabbi James A. Wax.

Chicago-born artist and rapper Marcellous Lovelace designed the colorful mural that represents the 1968 Sanitation Workers' Strike, in particular the iconic photograph captured by Richard L. Copley that shows striking workers holding "I AM A MAN" signs, a nod to the movement's demand for respect, safety, and equal pay for black sanitation employees in Memphis. The mural was installed in 2014 by BLK75 as part of the South Main Mosaic Artwalk, which

---

Paint Memphis facilitates huge mural projects in neighborhoods throughout the city. For more public art, check out its projects on the Chelsea Flood Wall, Martin Luther King Jr. Avenue, and others.

MEMPHIS UPSTANDERS

What: Mural featuring extraordinary Memphians

Where: 115 Huling Ave.

I AM A MAN

What: Mural depicting the 1968 Sanitation Workers' Strike

Where: 398 S. Main St.

I LOVE MEMPHIS MURALS

What: Series of murals created by local artists

Where: Nine locations in Memphis

includes a trail of murals and public art in the historic arts district.

In 2009 Memphis Tourism founded the *I Love Memphis* blog to increase civic pride and provide a local's view of the city's best assets. As a part of this mission, the I Love Memphis mural program launched in 2011 with a large red mural designed by artist Brandon Marshall in a high-traffic parking lot in Cooper-Young. To date, nine murals or billboards have been installed in neighborhoods around town. Some, like the Heart Bridge Crosstown mural designed by Kong Wee Pang and Jay Crum, are highly visible, and others are more hidden, such as *Abstract Love* by Jean Marie Burks across the street from Murphy's pub in Midtown.

MEET THE INDUCTEES

Where is the Memphis Music Hall of Fame?

In an upstairs space above the famous Lansky Brothers— "Clothier to the King"—you'll find a small but colorful museum dedicated to the most important people in Memphis music, past and present.

The Memphis Music Hall of Fame started in 2012 as a way to honor the musicians, bands, producers, and music industry professionals who created the Memphis sound across all genres. Each year, a group of Memphis music experts selects a diverse class of inductees who are celebrated in a ceremony and concert.

As of 2019 about sixty individuals and groups had been included. In 2015 the museum opened a physical location that music fans, Memphians, and visitors from around the world can explore. Though the space

---

MEMPHIS MUSIC HALL OF FAME

What: Artifacts from decades of Memphis music

Where: 126 Beale St.

Cost: Adults, $8; children 5–17, $6

Pro tip: Look for the Hard Rock Cafe at the corner of Beale and Second streets; the Memphis Music Hall of Fame is next to it.

Don't miss the Lansky Bros. shop downstairs from the Memphis Music Hall of Fame, where Elvis purchased many of his signature suits. The shop also sells memorabilia and t-shirts.

Memphis group Three 6 Mafia became the first rap group to ever win an Oscar. Their song "It's Hard Out Here For a Pimp" from the film Hustle and Flow won an Academy Award for Best Original Song in 2006. Items from that awards show are on display at the museum.

isn't expansive, it does include representation from most of the members of the Hall of Fame.

The museum displays some truly one-of-a-kind items, such as a Tom Ford suit that Justin Timberlake wore during his *20/20 Experience* tour, an Isaac Hayes keyboard, a pink velvet suit and cape worn by Rufus Thomas, Elvis's phone, plenty of videos, artifacts, and much more.

GOODBYE BLOCKBUSTER, HELLO BLACK LODGE

Does Memphis still have a video rental store?

Do you remember the excitement of going to your local video rental store on Friday nights? Do you recall the way you'd peruse the aisles, looking for the latest release, or at least a flick you hadn't seen before? Did you remember to rewind?

Today in Memphis, you can recreate this experience from the late twentieth century, with a modern edge, at the unique video rental store and event venue known as the Black Lodge.

Getting its name from the cult television program *Twin Peaks*, the first Black Lodge Video location was a Cooper-Young institution from 1999 to 2015. Located in a converted house on South Cooper, the video rental portion was several rooms with endless shelves of DVDs.

The store offered everything from current releases to classic films to more offbeat selections. Black Lodge set itself apart with its extensive collection of horror, B-movies, foreign films, and cult classics, not to mention its desire to stay open extra late. In 2015, citing the changing market, Black Lodge owner Matthew Martin had to leave the original Cooper-Young spot. After years of searching for the perfect location, Black Lodge was finally reborn in the fall of 2019 in the Crosstown

---

On the final evening that the original Black Lodge location was open, the owners hosted one of their raging parties—it sold out every single beer from the convenience store across the street.

The expert staff at Black Lodge can help you choose the perfect flick, from anime to cult classics to hard-to-find movies you won't find on the streaming services.

BLACK LODGE VIDEO

What: Old-school video rental store

Where: 405 Cleveland St.

Cost: $4 for five-day rental, or $10 a month for four DVDs at a time

Pro tip: The shop hosts a bad-movie night (with an official name we can't print here) every Sunday evening for night owls; expect weird, wacky, and disturbing flicks starting at 10 p.m.

neighborhood, not far from the Crosstown Concourse.

The collection of more than twenty thousand DVDs now sits in a sleek, renovated building with a large screen and a bar that hosts plenty of events, film screenings, concerts, and parties, in addition to renting out the well-curated collection that attracts serious film buffs. The original Black Lodge was known for its popular Halloween parties and alternative shows, a tradition that continues in the new location. The owners also help host the Time Warp Drive-In movie series at the Malco Summer Quartet Drive-In.

SOURCES

Hidden Cemetery In Midtown: Site visit; http://haywoodcountyline. blogspot.com/2012/06/i-found-some-family-buried-between-home. html; http://cremedememph.blogspot.com/2011/10/cemetery-behind-cash-saverpiggly-wiggly.html

Prince Mongo's Castle: https://abandonedsoutheast.com/2017/03/31/ prince-mongos-castle/; http://www.memphisheritage.org/ashlar-hall/

No Man's Land at Elmwood: Site visit and guided tour; https:// memphismagazine.com/ask-vance/the-martyrs-of-memphis-graves-elmwood-s-yellow-fever-victims/; https://www.frommers.com/ destinations/memphis/attractions/elmwood-cemetery

A Pink Palace: Site visit; http://historic-memphis.com/biographies/ pigglywiggly/pigglywiggly.html; https://www.memphismuseums.org/ about/history/

The Green Beetle: Interview with Savannah Shelton; https:// memphismagazine.com/ask-vance/the-green-beetles/; https://www. bluetoad.com/publication/?m=&i=94838&p=25&pp=1

The Labyrinth by the Tree of Life: Site visit; https://uacmem.org/ projects/tree-of-life; https://memphistn.gov/parks/parks/cancer_ survivors_park

Robert Church Park: https://memphisheritagetrail.com/project/robert-r-church-park/; http://www.historic-memphis.com/memphis-historic/ movietheaters/church.html

Phillips Recording Studio: https://samphillipsrecording.com/about/; https://www.youtube.com/watch?v=TzC2RkfipVI; https://www. memphistypehistory.com/visit-sam-phillips-recording-service/

Free Music at the Levitt Shell: Site visit; https://www.levittshell.org/ history; http://www.scottymoore.net/overton.html

First Baptist Beale Street: https://www.downtownmemphis.com/guide-to-downtown/historic-first-baptist-beale/; http://www.memphisheritage. org/first-baptist-church-beale-street-baptist-church/; https://www.pbs. org/blackpress/news_bios/wells.html

St. Jude's Hidden Garden: Site visit; Interview with Meghan Stuthard; https://www.stjude.org/about-st-jude/visit/tours/danny-and-rose-marie-thomas-memorial-garden.html

Elvis's Memphian Theater: Interview with Michael Detroit; http://www. historic-memphis.com/memphis-historic/movietheaters/memphian. html; https://www.youtube.com/watch?v=FLk9_zwMxzc

Caritas Village: Site visit; Interview with Jeff Hulett; https://caritasvillage. org/team; http://www.memphisdowntowner.com/my2cents-pages/ Onie-Johns.html; https://www.highgroundnews.com/features/ CaritasReopening.aspx

Tigers around Town: https://alumni.memphis.edu/s/1728/15/index. aspx?sid=1728&gid=2&pgid=547

It's 2 a.m. and We're at Alex's: https://www.commercialappeal. com/story/entertainment/dining/2019/11/12/memphis-restaurants-alexs-tavern-anniversary-rocky-kasaftes/2513914001/; http://www. bestmemphisburger.com/2011/08/08/alexs-tavern/

Meet Mary the Ghost: Site visit; Paranormal tour; https://www. strangerdimensions.com/2014/09/12/mary-ghost-orpheum-theatre/

Bass Pro Pyramid: Site visit; https://www.citylab.com/ design/2020/01/memphis-pyramid-history-bass-pro-shop-downtown-attractions/599806/

Hidden Jade Museum: Site visit; https://belzmuseum.org/our-collections/; https://www.atlasobscura.com/places/belz-museum-of-asian-and-judaic-art

Pioneer Springs Trail: Site visit; http://www.shelbyfriends.org/; https:// rootsrated.com/stories/complete-guide-to-meeman-shelby-forest-state-park

Crystal Shrine Grotto: Site visit; https://memphismagazine.com/culture/ the-secrets-of-crystal-shrine-grotto/

Mid-South Coliseum: Site visit; Tour and Interview with Marvin Stockwell; https://focusmidsouth.com/blog/original-memphis-mid-south-coliseum/; http://www.memphisheritage.org/mid-south-coliseum/; Hall, Ron, and Sherman Willmott. Memphis Rocks! a Concert History, 1955-1985. Memphis, TN: Shangri-la Projects, 2014.

Chisca Hotel: http://historic-memphis.com/memphis-historic/hotels/ hotels.html; https://styleblueprint.com/memphis/everyday/chisca-launching-elvis-luxury-living/

The Peabody's Secret Room: Site visit; http://www.scottymoore.net/ article551122.html; https://www.peabodymemphis.com/history

The Man in Black: Site visit; https://www.memphisflyer.com/MusicBlog/ archives/2019/06/11/ceremony-to-celebrate-johnny-cash-statue-by-mike-mccarthy; https://cooperyoung.org/cash-statue-effort-passes-halfway-mark/; https://www.memphisflyer.com/MusicBlog/ archives/2019/06/11/ceremony-to-celebrate-johnny-cash-statue-by-mike-mccarthy

Lucky Heart Cosmetics: Site visit; https://luckyheart.com/; https://www. highgroundnews.com/features/LuckyHeart.aspx

Silky's Irish Diving Goats: https://www.memphistypehistory.com/goats/; http://silkyosullivans.com/; https://www.memphisflyer.com/memphis/q-and-a-with-thomas-silky-sullivan/Content?oid=3365426

Metal Museum Gates: Site visit; https://www.metalmuseum.org/ anniversary-gates

The Wonder of the Wolf: Site visit; https://www.tn.gov/environment/ program-areas/na-natural-areas/natural-areas-west-region/west-region/ghost-river.html; https://wolfriver.org/

Botanic Garden Brood: Site visit; tour with Mary Helen Butler; https:// www.memphisbotanicgarden.com/buzz/posts/backyard-chickens

Birthplace of a Legend: Site visit; https://www.roadsideamerica.com/ story/34301; https://www.citylab.com/design/2018/08/whats-going-on-with-aretha-franklins-birth-house-in-memphis/567922/

Legacy of Georgia Tann: https://nypost.com/2017/06/17/this-woman-stole-children-from-the-poor-to-give-to-the-rich/; https://www. commercialappeal.com/story/news/2018/06/11/victims-tennessee-childrens-home-society-adoption-scandal-involving-georgia-tann-share-their-stor-4/682152002/

A Daring Rescue: Site visit; https://memphismagazine.com/ features/tom-lee-a-heros-tale/; https://www.wmcactionnews5.com/ story/38506265/tom-lee-memorial-could-be-removed-from-park/

Take a Picture with Little Milton: https://www.americanbluesscene. com/statue-of-little-milton-takes-a-seat-in-front-of-the-blues-hall-of-fame-in-advance-of-may-8-opening/; https://www.vintagevinylnews. com/2015/04/statue-of-little-milton-installed-at.html; https://blues. org/hall-of-fame-museum/

A Grand Carousel: https://cmom.com/explore/exhibits/grand-carousel/; http://www.memphisheritage.org/libertyland-grand-carousel/; Stevenson, John R, and Jimmy Ogle. 2017. Libertyland. Charleston, SC: Arcadia Publishing.

Tune In to Ditty TV: Site visit; Interview with Amy Wright; https://dittytv. com/about/; https://www.washingtonpost.com/lifestyle/magazine/ they-left-dcs-tech-scene-for-memphis--and-started-dittytv-a-streaming- channel-for-roots-music/2020/03/02/f83f27c0-41ee-11ea-b503- 2b077c436617_story.html

The Blue House on Beale Street: http://www.bealestreet.com/wc-handy- museum; https://memphismusichalloffame.com/inductee/wchandy/

Memphis Buffaloes: Interview with Angie Whitfield and Rebecca Dailey; https://www.shelbyfarmspark.org/our-buffalo-herd

Before Graceland: Site visit with Backbeat Tours; https:// ilovememphisblog.com/2011/08/24-hours-of-elvis-608-p-m-elvis-slept- here/; https://maps.roadtrippers.com/us/memphis-tn/accommodation/ lauderdale-courts-memphis

Rock 'n' Soul Museum: Site visit; https://www.memphisrocknsoul.org/ exhibits; https://www.memphisrocknsoul.org/smithsonian

The House of Mews: https://memphismagazine.com/features/columns/ an-interview-with-elain-harvey-house-of-mews/

Chickasaw Mounds: https://www.chickasaw.net/Our-Nation/ History/Europeans-Contact.aspx; http://www.memphisheritage.org/ chickasaw-heritage-park-de-soto-park/; https://www.waymarking.com/ waymarks/WMNJY4_Chickashaw_Heritage_Park_Memphis_TN; https:// dailymemphian.com/article/70/The-Chickasaw-Nations-role-in-the- founding-of-Memphis

Sex Pistols Taco Bell: https://www.memphisflyer.com/FlyontheWallBlog/ archives/2017/01/06/its-sex-pistols-taco-bell-day-in-memphis-eat-a- burrito; http://www.guerrillamonsterfilms.com/memphis/sex-pistols/ index.html

Clayborn Temple: Interview with Steve Fox; https://clayborn-temple.org/; https://civilrightstrail.com/attraction/clayborn-temple/

Meet Elmer at the Dixon: Site visit; Interview with Kristen Rambo and Dixon staff; https://www.dixon.org/about

Hattiloo Theatre: https://hattiloo.org/our-history/; https://www. theroot.com/the-memphis-theater-thats-performing-blackness- unapolog-1835490209

Underground Railroad Slave Haven: http://slavehavenmemphis.com/; https://www.memphisflyer.com/backissues/issue419/cvr419.htm

Royal Studios: http://www.royalstudios.com/history; https://www. memphisdailynews.com/news/2015/jan/23/legendary-memphis-studio- has-no-1-hit-with-uptown-funk/

Secrets of Rhodes College: Site visit; Interview with J. Dylan Sandifer; https://www.rhodes.edu/about-rhodes/our-campus

The Goodwill Station: https://civilrightstrail.com/attraction/wdia-radio-station/; https://www.blackpast.org/african-american-history/wdia-radio-station-1947/

Garage Rock Pilgrimage :https://www.goner-records.com/gonerfest/gf13-history.html; https://americansongwriter.com/velvet-ditch-blues-goner-records-history-memphis-punk/eileen-townsend/

Altown Skate Park: Site visit; Interview with John Younger; https://www.memphisflyer.com/memphis/build-skate-repeat/Content?oid=3425434

See the Big Kids: https://ilovememphisblog.com/2012/02/365-things-to-do-in-memphis-55-see-the-big-kids/; http://dlynx.rhodes.edu:8080/jspui/handle/10267/26377; https://www.memphisflyer.com/memphis/big-kids/Content?oid=2783872

US Marine Hospital: https://abandonedsoutheast.com/2016/05/16/marine-hospital/; https://www.memphisflyer.com/memphis/an-inside-look-into-the-us-marine-hospital/Content?oid=3709579; https://www.metalmuseum.org/history; http://www.memphisheritage.org/u-s-marine-hospital-executive-building-laundry-kitchen/map-us-marine-hospital/

The Six-Story Mural: Interview with Michael Roy; https://ilovememphisblog.com/2016/07/whats-going-on-in-this-huge-new-mural-downtown/

Ride A Trolley: https://www.commercialappeal.com/story/news/local/2018/02/27/mata-approves-free-fares-first-two-weeks-main-street-trolleys-return/374913002/; http://www.gomacotrolley.com/Resources/pages/birney_memphis.html

Explore the Crosstown Concourse: Site visit; https://crosstownconcourse.com/updates/amazon-before-amazon; https://crosstownconcourse.com/about

Views at the River Garden: Site visit; https://www.memphisriverparks.org/

Bluesman on Beale: https://memphismusichalloffame.com/inductee/wchandy/; https://historic-memphis.com/biographies/wchandy/handy.html

Browse in Burke's Books: https://www.burkesbooks.com/about.php

A Vinyl Paradise: Site visit; Interview with John Miller; https://magazine.vinylmeplease.com/magazine/shangri-la-records-best-record-store-tennessee/; https://shangri.com/about/

Making Music in Memphis: Site visit; Tour with Brandon Seavers; https://dailymemphian.com/section/suburbsbartlett/article/2869/Bartlett-business-is-finding-a-market-for-vinyl-records

Captain Harris House: http://cooperyoung.weebly.com/captainharrishouse.html; http://www.memphisheritage.org/captain-harris-house/

Let's Do The Time Warp Again: Site visit; facebook.com/timewarpdrivein

Reviving The Memphis Spirit: Site visit; https://olddominick.com/timeline/

Martyrs Park: Site visit; https://memphistn.gov/parks/parks/historical_and_special_parks

Beale Street Landing: Site visit; https://www.downtownmemphis.com/guide-to-downtown/beale-street-landing/; https://memphisriverboats.net/; https://www.americanqueensteamboatcompany.com/

Remember Natch the Bear: Interview with Zoo staff; https://www.memphiszoo.org/history

Lady Liberty, Memphis Edition: https://www.nytimes.com/2006/07/05/us/05liberty.html, https://worldovercomers.org/statue-liberation/

The Withers Collection: Site visit; https://www.thewitherscollection.com/about; https://www.latimes.com/archives/la-xpm-2007-oct-18-me-withers18-story.html

Downtown's Antique Mysteries: Site visits and tours; https://molliefontainelounge.com/; https://www.downtownmemphis.com/neighborhoods/victorian-village/; http://victorianvillageinc.org/; https://www.woodruff-fontaine.org/; https://www.memphismuseums.org/historic-houses/

Soul Food in Soulsville: https://www.commercialappeal.com/story/entertainment/dining/reviews/2018/03/29/four-way-oldest-soul-food-town/454322002/; https://memphismagazine.com/food/rightly-seasoned/

Little Tea Shop: Site visit; https://www.memphisflyer.com/memphis/a-documentary-on-little-tea-shop-is-in-the-works/Content?oid=21380463; http://www.mortimersrestaurant.net/?page_id=2

Mason Temple: Site visit; Tour with Carolyn Michael-Banks; https://www.nps.gov/nr/travel/civilrights/tn1.htm; https://civilrightstrail.com/attraction/mason-temple-church-of-god-in-christ/

Memphis Slim House: http://memphisslimhouse.org/about-memphis-slim/; https://memphismusichalloffame.com/inductee/memphisslim/; https://memphismagazine.com/home-garden/memphis-slim-house/

Cornelia's Words: http://womenofachievement.org/heritage/cornelia-crenshaw/; https://www.highgroundnews.com/features/CorneliaCrenshawLibrary.aspx; https://memphisheritagetrail.com/

Soul Women: Interview with Jayne Ellen White; https://memphismusichalloffame.com/inductee/jimstewartestelleaxton/; https://www.huffpost.com/entry/the-woman-behind-the-memp_b_5729242http://www.alcenias.com/about-us.html

One-Stop Cultural Shop: Site visit; https://www.southernfolklore.com/history; https://choose901.com/center-for-southern-folklore/

The Antenna: https://www.memphisflyer.com/memphis/the-antenna-club-redux/Content?oid=1590578; https://www.facebook.com/pages/Antenna-Club/277174642381067; https://m.memphisflyer.com/SingAllKinds/archives/2014/07/24/ross-johnson-remembers-the-antenna-club

A Haunted Brothel on Main Street: https://www.thrillist.com/eat/memphis/earnestine-and-hazels-memphis-burger-dive-bar; https://earnestineandhazelsjukejoint.com/about-us/the-bar/; https://www.vice.com/en_us/article/vvxnmb/this-is-what-its-like-to-work-at-the-most-haunted-bar-in-america

Egyptian Connection: https://www.latimes.com/archives/la-xpm-1987-02-01-mn-319-story.html; https://www.memphis.edu/egypt/; https://wreg.com/news/photos-ramses-ii-statue-moved-to-u-of-m/

The Pinch District: Site visit; https://www.downtownmemphis.com/neighborhoods/the-pinch/; http://www.alcenias.com/about-us.html; http://www.memphisheritage.org/pinch-north-main-historic-district/

Model of the Mighty Mississippi: Site visit; https://storyboardmemphis.com/memphis-history/history-memphis-city-planning/mud-island-history-part/; https://www.memphistravel.com/trip-ideas/lets-go-see-mud-island-river-park

Hot Rods in the Edge: Site visit; Tour with Stewart Kerby; https://www.edgemotormuseum.com/

Overton Park Old Forest: https://overtonpark.org/2016/08/04/walk-and-learn-on-the-old-forest-loop/; https://www.tufc.com/project/old-forest-of-overton-park/

Machine Gun Kelly's Last Hideout: http://obscurememphis-thecitysbestkeptsecrets.com/index.php/machine-gun-kelly-homelandmarks/; https://memphismagazine.com/features/machine-gun-kelly-memphis-public-enemy/

Tragedy at the Lorraine: Site visit; https://www.civilrightsmuseum.org/; https://www.nps.gov/places/tennessee-the-lorraine-hotel-memphis.htm

The Influence of Ardent: https://www.ardentstudios.com/history-2; https://www.billboard.com/articles/news/6413860/ardent-studios-founder-john-fry-dies-at-69; https://www.rollingstone.com/music/music-news/alex-chilton-set-to-go-243920/

A Memphis Art Tour: Site visits; https://engage.facinghistory.org/mural/; https://ilovememphisblog.com/2014/10/the-state-of-the-mural-address-your-weekend-mission/; https://www.memphisdailynews.com/news/2014/sep/30/neighborhood-art/

Meet the Inductees: Site visit; https://memphismusichalloffame.com/museum/

Goodbye Blockbuster, Hello Black Lodge: Site visit; https://www.commercialappeal.com/story/news/2019/09/12/black-lodge-memphis-video-rental-store-crosstown-concourse/2289626001/; https://blacklodgememphis.com/

INDEX